# Praise for Sanaya's Writings

Sanaya's words are so perfect every day. It seems as though she knows what is going on in my life, and her message is exactly what I need to hear. Sanaya is of utmost importance in my life.

*Ann W.*

Each day Sanaya sets the high flying happiness tone of my day. Reading Sanaya keeps me in a place of love for not only myself but everyone I come into contact with. Sanaya is my personal reality check.

*Nancy N.*

Two years ago my beloved wife Victoria passed on from cancer. Not long after her passing I began reading daily messages from Sanaya. These messages from Spirit quickly became a form of daily meditation for me, a source of strength, insight and hope as I work through grief and gain an ever greater sense of Victoria's spirit beside me every hour of every day.

*Bill H.*

It never ceases to amaze me that no matter what date Sanaya's message came through it is always perfect for the day I am reading it! A day without the messages is an incomplete day.

*Libby S.*

Sanaya's daily messages are simple, yet profound. I list the ones that are pertinent to me on my *Evernote* account and review them daily. My spirit becomes more and more elevated as I feel my soul growing, and my heart singing.

Kurt C.

Also by Suzanne Giesemann:


*Messages of Hope*

*Love Beyond Words*

*The Priest and the Medium*

*The Real Alzheimer's*

*Conquer Your Cravings*

*Living a Dream*

*It's Your Boat Too*


Co-Authored with Janet Nohavec:

*Through the Darkness*

*Where Two Worlds Meet*

# IN THE SILENCE

*365 Days of Inspiration from Spirit*

*Suzanne Giesemann*

Published by One Mind Books, www.OneMindBooks.com

Cover and interior design by Elisabeth Giesemann

Library of Congress Control Number: 2013919570

Library of Congress Cataloging-in-Publication Data

In the Silence: 365 Days of Inspiration from Spirit/Suzanne Giesemann

ISBN: 978-0-9838539-3-0

Printed in the United States of America

# *Acknowledgements*

Nothing opens the heart more fully than gratitude, and my heart overflows frequently these days.

My husband, Ty, continues to bless me with his unwavering love and support. I need only think of him when I sit to give thanks, and I am drawn immediately to that sacred place within my heart where love dwells.

This book would not exist were it not for my wonderful friend and assistant, Bev Garlipp. The extra vibration of love on each page is the result of Bev having carefully selected and formatted each entry from over a year's worth of possibilities. Her idea to index each message by topic now allows you, the reader, to find just the right words when they are needed.

Thanks to my step-daughter, Elisabeth, for her stunning cover design. She has captured exactly the feeling I envisioned to accompany Spirit's inspiring words.

And finally, thank you to God and to Sanaya, who has never failed to guide me when I don't know which way to turn, and whose universal messages of love show all of us how to find the light within us.

# *Preface*

When Sanaya spoke to me for the first time during my morning meditation on August 1st, 2010, the powerful presence was unmistakable. "Who are you?" I asked. The voice spoke to me in the third person plural, using the pronoun "we" and explained that "they" were the collective consciousness of all of my guides.

"You are to call us Sanaya," they said. "And you should prepare to write and write and write as we give you words of wit and wisdom each day."

They (or "she" as many of Sanaya's followers now call her) have given me words to write each day ever since. The messages invariably cover topics dealing with our interconnectedness and the love that binds us all. Sanaya shares advice about our common struggles and how to find peace in the midst of chaos. She is infinitely patient and understanding, and never judgmental. Rarely do the messages use the word "should," but they frequently give one pause for thought and lovingly point the way to better choices.

More than once I listened as a radio host or a church pastor read one of Sanaya's messages aloud to their audience. It was as if I were hearing the words for the first time, and I thought, "Wow, that's beautiful!" And each time the thought was reinforced, "That didn't come from me."

Sanaya's words provide evidence of how much we are loved and guided by those in spirit. Because the truths shared are universal, followers of Sanaya often relate that a message was "sent just for them".

I take no credit for the messages' wisdom. When Sanaya speaks through me I am in a deep meditative state. I write the words as fast as they come and later type them after returning to full consciousness. Often when someone asks me what Sanaya spoke about that day I can't remember. This is because the messages don't come from my own consciousness. Sanaya speaks from a higher dimension than our own.

The messages included here are all new since the publication of the first collection, *Love Beyond Words*. Some of the entries were selected because they were named as favorites by readers of my daily blog, SanayaSays.com. Some were selected because they received special comments from readers on my Facebook page. All were selected with Spirit's guidance.

There is no time in Sanaya's world, and the advice given here is timeless. However, to organize the messages, each has been assigned a day of the year. Repetition is an excellent teacher, and Sanaya knows we need to hear the messages many times using different analogies until the truth sinks in and becomes part of our conscious mind. In the index I have listed the messages by the key lessons or topics covered.

There are many ways to read Sanaya's words and one is no better than another. Follow your heart. You may wish to read each day in order. You may feel a need to read the messages associated with a certain issue or question you are dealing with, or you may be led by Spirit to simply open the book to a particular page. Every word is given to us in love, is written with love, and holds the energy of love.

May you feel that love as you read, and may you be inspired to share that higher vibration with others as you go about your day.

## IN THE SILENCE

Life is a series of decisions
You must make.
Do I do this or don't I?
Which road should I take?

You never know the answers
Until you clear the mind.
And then there in the silence
The purest guidance you will find.

It's there you feel the Presence
With the softness of a dove
That comes alive inside your heart
The gift of God's pure love.

It brings you to a knowing
That you need not fear a fall
For now you've found the wings to fly
And rise above it all.

*January 2*

## FINDING THE SANCTUARY

When turmoil surrounds you, find the peace within yourself. You need not escape to a quiet sanctuary in some physical location, but to the quiet sanctuary inside the mind. "Oh, but I cannot quiet the mind," you say, and that is where you err.

Follow the breath into the silence. Set aside the chattering mind by giving it something else to focus upon but for a few moments. Say to yourself, "I am peace ..." and stretch out that sibilant sound at the end of the word on the exhalation. Now, say, "And I am love," feeling it as you pull it within your very soul on the inhalation. Take a few more breaths and say, "And all is well."

Breathe deeply and slowly and repeat these phrases. Place the tiniest of smiles upon your face as you do this meditation, thus releasing the tension in the face. And there you have it—your sanctuary. Go there often in the new year and peace will be the reward.

It is a choice, this thing called your state of mind. Seek it often and peace you will find.

## NOT EVEN TRYING

Why is it necessary to be still to hear the voice of God? The human is programmed to be busy. This is not part of your spiritual make-up, but a cultural learning.

There are cultures that accept stillness as a rite, knowing that this will bring communion with the Self. Yours is a culture that values doing over being, accomplishing over inner knowing. You can only know Truth by not accomplishing anything. Trying is counterproductive. Even in your attempts to reach a state of stillness you exert effort. Pay attention: Are you breathing with effort, or allowing the breaths to simply flow?

Surrender and allow yourself to be breathed. Take time throughout your day to simply be. Then and there in the silence and in perfect flow with the rhythm of the unforced breath will you hear the Voice. Allow it to be heard—not so still and small, but loud and clear once you have cleared the way through non-effort.

# *January 4*

## ARISE!

Why are you here? It is quite easy to go about each day in a robotic fashion. You have your routines. You get out of bed and take care of the body, washing, clothing, and feeding it. And then you entertain or exercise it perhaps, and do some work to make sure you can continue to entertain and feed and clothe it some more.

What is it all for? It is for the experience, my friend. Never forget this. And how will you spend each moment of this experience in your mind: absently or with awareness? Will you be focused always on the next action or will you fill each present action with the true purpose of life?

You are here to experience life in human form and to remember that this is not who you are eternally. You are spirit having a human experience. You are here to grow as a spirit—the part that never ceases growing. That part of you is all Love. If you can infuse love-awareness into each present moment whilst caring for the body, whilst working, exercising, and resting, we daresay you will vault from being in a robotic state to one of full interaction between the true Self and the present physical reality.

Expanded awareness is a beautiful state. Arise! Arise each day with a sense of purpose. Be the presence of Love and bring that Presence to all you do. Peace be upon you as you begin a new chapter of your Experience.

January 5

## THE GIFT OF DISCERNMENT

Do you remember as a child the excitement you did feel at the thought of a special holiday? If you believed in the one known as Santa Claus, did this thought not make your limbs tingle? This was a physical phenomenon brought about by the higher vibrations of joy. Do you realize that you can experience these same higher vibrations in the body through the act of reading spiritual literature?

Words are imbued with the energy of the source of the words. Think of the most Holy Scriptures around your world. If you truly attune to the vibrations of the words, you can feel an upsurge in the energy within when the words speak Truth. This is discernment.

These words you read now come from a higher source. Can you feel it? Read one of your murder mysteries. Do you feel it then? We think not. Pay attention. Choose a section of holy scripture and savor it slowly, looking for the true meaning. Do you feel a quickening? Is there a spread of warmth in your heart?

Pause now as we send you love in this very moment for your good intentions of soul-growth by joining with us and reading these words. It is like your Santa Claus coming down the chimney, is it not? Bearing gifts for you as you read. Blessed one, open your heart and accept this gift of eternal love.

*January 6*

## HOW MUCH YOU ARE LOVED

When you gaze upon a mountain, that is how much you are loved. When you see a beautiful flower or hear the most melodious song, that is how much you are loved. When you behold a newborn child and your heart opens wide, that is how much you are loved.

We cannot show you the full Force of how much you are loved or you would fall to your knees and be unable to function. That is how much you are loved … that much and more than you have yet experienced. Combine all of the instances you have experienced of loving another— of loving all others—and you will begin to get a taste of how much you are loved.

The amount you love yourself is infinitesimal compared to how much you are cared for, Beloved. Open your heart to this love and heal. Open your heart to this love and grow. Open your heart to this love and blossom. Be Loved.

.

## IN THE FACE OF CHAOS

You live in an orderly universe. Your planets follow orderly, predictable paths. The sun always rises and sets. Where there is seeming chaos in nature, there is actually an underlying order. Study your fractals and you will understand this.

At a personal level, you may experience chaos in your life, but on the grand scale order prevails. It is the Law of Life. You do not have the big picture at this time. There is a reason for that as well. You learn to come to a place of peace within the chaos, and that is part of the Plan.

Can you find peace at any time without having the big picture? It is a choice. Peace always lies within, where chaos cannot enter. Go there often—your true home.

# January 8

## THERE YOU ARE!

Do not devalue the worth of any other, for in so doing, you are belittling God. Once again, we remind you that all is of the Creator. What you see as the human part you know as individuality, but it is merely a creative, individualized aspect of the Creator, expressing with the free will with which it is endowed. Such beauty! Such Love does give it this human experience. The humanness may mask the beauty and love, but only, only, my friend, in your perception.

See past the humanness to the Spirit. See God, the Love behind the thoughts and actions, no matter how far they may seem to you from your limited view of God. Look upon another and rejoice, saying, "Oh, God! There you are!"

If you truly knew what you were seeing, you would either drop to your knees or run up and embrace the other. Look upon all others anew today and rejoice. Honor thy neighbor and honor thyself. It is all God.

*

## MASTERY

A jack of all trades, a master of none. It is good to be talented at many things, but is there benefit in mastery? Indeed, there is. You are here to achieve mastery over your thoughts.

When you can choose love and peace in every instant – yes, <u>every</u> instant, then you have achieved mastery. Until then, you dabble. Dabbling is well and good, as long as you do not play with your finger paints too long. Remember that the Master Artist is already within you.

At some point you will move on from dabbling, pick up your finest brushes, and create your masterpiece. It will not have random splotches of love and peace, but will be a glorious exposition of the finest artistry. The Master is inside. Learning to master your emotions is an art. What will you paint today?

*January 10*

## CONSTANT GROWTH

Throw away your childish things. We ask you to examine those thoughts and behaviors which are holding you firmly rooted in a particular vibration and are impeding your growth. What is it in you that is childish in the sense of an unevolved soul? Is it the need to defend yourself when wronged? Is it the act of lashing out when another is less than loving? Is it the need to judge or criticize?

All of these are behaviors of the ego, and along the spectrum of behaviors, these are indeed childish. We imply no judgment in this word. We simply use this term to awaken you to behaviors you would expect from a soul who is just awakening.

All are growing—yes, even beyond the grave—and a little awareness never hurts, does it? If it hurts, then throw away your childish things and remember who you are

## TRUTH OF MOTHER AND FATHER

The one true Mother is the One who birthed the spirit. Any other you identified as mother who failed to live up to an ideal was chosen as a teacher.

The one true Father is the one who birthed you as spirit. Any other you labeled as father is one you chose to serve as a teacher, and vice-versa. If you are disappointed in the ones you identified as mother or father, it is because you set an ideal based upon a belief system you learned. Were you adopted several times you would shift allegiances and perhaps hold onto the belief that the biological mother and father held the solution to your struggles. This is a falsehood.

Your human parents are fellow sojourners, here to learn. Have compassion for them as well as for yourself. There is one true Source of Love and Comfort and it lies within you. You are an aspect of that eternal Source of Love. Give up the belief in a mother and father who are separate from you. Send love and gratitude to the very human beings you formerly believed were your source for the lessons you shared together.

Now, allow yourself to feel the loving arms of the true Mother/Father as you receive from within what you have been searching for outside of yourself your whole human life.

.

*January 12*

## AMID THE SORROW

Sorrow seems to last forever, but it does not. It is a process. What is a process, but a series of steps one experiences to reach a goal. In the case of sorrow, what could possibly be the goal? Growth, understanding, surrender, greater love ... all of these are outcomes of having loved and supposedly lost it, or having experienced some event which lacked love.

You have a positive experience and wish to remain in that state. When the state changes, sorrow is the result. To get back to the original state, you go through the process, but lo, the end result is an expanded state in which you are stronger. You have learned things about yourself. You have made new connections. You have survived. You are still here. And in this expanded state come new opportunities for love. They may differ from your past experiences, and there is a reason for this: the soul has grown. There was a reason for your sorrow.

Find the purpose in your sorrow. The process need not last forever. Only the soul does that. Only love is real and lasting. Carry this thought with you as you process the process of growth.

*January 13*

## BELIEVE!

Believe. This is all we ask of you. Why is it so difficult for you to loosen the tight bonds you have wrapped around your view of reality? Do you fear ridicule? Do you fear that you will have to change? Do you know how your life will change when you open your mind to the possibility of a reality beyond that which you see, hear, and touch? We believe you do, and we wish to tell you that you have nothing to fear.

Escape from your self-imposed prison. Break free of the bonds and step into the world of make BELIEVE. Yes, it is magical beyond your wildest dreams. Is this not what you dream of—a fairy-tale land of beauty and love? It is real, and it can be here for you now. Step inside and let the adventure begin. It begins with belief.

# *January 14*

## PERFECT IN EVERY WAY

Perfection comes at a price. Striving, always striving. Forsaking others. Anxiety. And what is this elusive thing you seek? Does it even exist? It is a goal you set to be flawless or to perform flawlessly, but who is it that determines what is a flaw and what is not? Do you see the folly in this striving?

In the human world there is no state of perfection. Yes, it is good to aim high. Yes, it is most advisable to raise the bar from previous achievements. In this way you grow, but aiming for a goal which is ever elusive only leads to frustration and disappointment.

Aim to love yourself. Aim for excellence in all that you do. Aim to be good and kind to all you meet. Do you see the perfection in that? A bit of a paradox, perhaps, this concept of perfection. Do not miss our meaning by splitting hairs with your words. We merely wish you to go easy on yourself whilst still aiming to grow. To grow in what? In being the manifestation and expression of Love in your world.

## JOY LIVES IN THE NOW

Come in from the rain.
No longer suffer pain.
It's time to dry the tears
That have plagued you all these years.

So many suffer sorrow.
Afraid to face the morrow.
They hold onto the past
Where painful memories last.

The joy lies not ahead,
When there you look with dread.
Nor does it lie behind
Where the memories remind.

The joy lives in the now.
In this moment you find how
To open up to Truth itself
'Tis the way to peace and health.

The joy so naturally follows
The one whose pain he swallows
And surrounds it with the Light
No longer filled with fright.

Free now to simply live
And in this moment give
The present its full due
By stepping into the real you.

*January 16*

## IN THE FACE OF A STORM

You are preparing for a storm. What do you do? You place heavy boards over large windows. You pick up objects which could fly about. All of these are protective measures. Do you not see that often you prepare yourself in the same way in your mind for coming storms? You close the shutters around yourself, thus closing yourself off from interaction with others. No love can get in or out. You have left nothing lying around your "yard," so completely insulated are you by this perceived threat.

So, another may rant and howl. What is the best reaction? To howl back, to shutter yourself inside, or to radiate such a brilliant light that it quells the storm? You know the answer. Open wide your shutters and let your love shine. Always light will overcome darkness. Simply remain calm, trusting completely in the Light, and you will be guided safely along your path.

## THE GRAND REALITY

You currently perceive the world through your five senses, for this is where you place your attention. But does not a dog perceive the world differently? Yes, for it sees not the same colors as you do due to different physical receptors within the eye. And does not a plant perceive the world differently? Yes, for it has no eyes at all. Yet all have Consciousness. All beings perceive reality differently based on their method of perceiving. For each individual, perception is truly their reality.

So, what is truly real? What is the one thing that never changes? Step back behind the perceiver. Who or what is perceiving the perceiver? There is only One Mind. How boring would be existence if there were only one experience. Instead, the One Mind has fragmented itself into billions and billions of focuses of consciousness to perceive its creation from every possible angle. Yours is one. Your neighbor's is another. Your cat's is another. And in that diversity, the Great Creator rejoices and enjoys. So, rejoice and enjoy your reality today. You are co-creating in a grand way.

Isn't it truly grand to be a part of the One?

*January 18*

## ATTRACTION IN ACTION

Visualize success and it is yours,
For from your thoughts success it pours.
It's when you doubt, that then you fail
For thoughts of doubt will then prevail.

You do become that which you see
For in your mind your thoughts run free.
Thoughts are things; know this now.
To understand this, we'll show you how:

Hold an image in your mind…
The clearest picture that you can find.
Surround it now with thoughts of success.
Do not allow in anything less.

Nurture this image in the days ahead.
Think of it as you lie in your bed.
And when you awaken and get on with your day.
On naught but success should you then pray.

But sit not back and fail to act.
Remember this important fact.
Together with Spirit you co-create.
To be weak and helpless is not your fate.

.

OUTSIDE THE BOX

Do not berate yourself for not going along with the crowd. Do you realize how many do so because they have learned that this is the route to approval? Always follow your heart and your instincts. If these lead you down a solo path, so be it. You are an individual. Does this fly in the face of oneness? Not at all.

Have we not taught you repeatedly that you are an individual focus of the Source? Quite so. If all of God's creations did this or that merely to go along with the crowd, where would be the learning? Where would be the growth? These take place from those with the courage to step outside the box and be different.

Express your individuality. Be bold and adventurous. It is okay to think of the self every now and then instead of the group. Come from a place of love, and always you will make a good choice.

*January 20*

## LIVING WITH LOSS

Sorrow is a necessary step to healing. You need not stay in that state, but it does help to recognize it. What comes next is up to you. It is you who transmutes the lower energy and raises it to a more comfortable place. There are no timelines for overcoming grief and loss. It is a process of learning and adjusting, and then deciding what is the best way to live in the present moment.

All of life is about change. When things change, there is loss. Nothing lasts forever but the soul. When you can come to terms with this fact and not hold on so dearly to the past, you can flood your present with healing love and compassion for all others. All suffer loss. All need love. No one bypasses the route to the soul. Flood your world with love and help to ease the suffering.

## THE RACE

You look upon the grass that's green.
With envy you do gaze.
In doing so what's in between
Appears as if in haze.

How often do you overlook
What's right before your eyes?
Your life is like an open book
Yet to you the end's the prize.

The race belongs not to the swift,
Not to the one who gets there first.
Each moment is a golden gift
Savored slowly, not run all in one burst.

Relax, you'll get there when you see
There's no end, just here and now.
To know this is to be set free.
So just surrender and allow.

*January 22*

## RUNGS

Steps on a ladder ... that is where you stand each moment. All of life is about climbing that ladder ever closer to the highest rung. Your Source resides upon every rung, but you feel It the most and have the most all-encompassing view from the top.

Meanwhile, as you climb you will leave some beings at the lower rungs and encounter others on those higher. One rung is not better or worse than another. These different levels merely represent greater awakening.

Have compassion for those whose view is not yet all-encompassing. They are on the self-same journey. The climb is not always easy. Help them along, but aim always for the next rung. Be satisfied, yes. Know that you may slip back to a lower rung from time to time, but always will there be a loving hand reaching down to help you ascend higher.

## FOCUS

It is a miracle that you are here. Look at your earth, how it supports you with the exact temperature range, the exact nutrients, fuels, and oxygen your body needs to exist You could not survive if any of these parameters were changed just a bit.

Look at the body that supports the spirit that is you—a miraculous machine of interconnected, cooperating parts. It is a miracle in motion. Look at the miracle of conception, growth, and birth. The perfection is astounding.

Look around you today and see the miraculous. It is all around you, yet you so often focus on the mundane. Focus on the big and small miracles today and feel your heart expanding with love, for it is Love which has engendered all of the miracles, and the greatest of these is you.

# January 24

## UNDERSTANDING ONENESS

If you could see with your eyes the pure spirit of those around you, you would never again struggle with the concept of oneness. All you would see is a bright white light. Where once you saw Dick and Jane and Dick and Jane's clothing, shape, size, and features, now you would see not the human, but the spirit—the light. No longer would there be difference, but love, blending and melding with no separation. Where does light end? It does not.

Even after you pass, there continues to be differentiation in the form of vibration, which manifests as sound and color to those who see such things. But the closer to pure Love the spirit grows, the closer to pure white light it becomes. Picture those around you in their essential form as white light. It is always there, for it comes not from outside, but lies within. Picture this radiating from all those around you and from within yourself as well, and you will begin to understand oneness.

## BENDING

At times you waver. This is doubt. Doubt comes from being human and is understandable.

Have compassion for the side of you that forgets to trust. And then, into your life come angels, in the form of messengers who carry just the right words to put you back on track. You hear their words and once again stand tall and firm in your awareness of who you are. Now, once again, you are strong.

And so it goes, this game of bending in the wind like the tall tree. There is no shame in this. It is for this reason that you are created to be flexible and not break when you waver. We will continue to send you messengers until you no longer need them.

That is Love. Spread it around.

*January 26*

## THROROUGHLY LOVEABLE

Why do you not love yourself as we do? Do you think you are not worthy? We love you without conditions, without judgment. You are so very precious to us, to All That Is. Yet, you do not see this. Why? Because you have been judged in the past by those who raised you. You have been told what to think. And now you judge others and they continue to judge you.

This is a human trait. See beyond that. Cease projecting human traits and see yourself and others as we do ... as tiny babes, free of flaws, thoroughly loveable. Babies make mistakes. Do you love them any less? You are so thoroughly loved, so thoroughly cherished. Project that upon others and it will come back to you.

## WHAT DIFFERENCE?

A cat or dog dies, and you grieve. A beloved pet gone from your life. Others may not understand. "How can you be so sad? It was only an animal!" In this we correct you. It was the object of love. It was a source of love. Was it any less valuable than a human being in this regard? You place value on objects in your life in such a curious way.

Life is about learning to love and appreciate all living things as manifestations of Love. If a cat or a dog teaches you this lesson, what a gift you have been given! Some learn to love through their animal companions far more than through their human companions. What difference? Love is love. Love is Life itself. Value all Life equally, and love with all your heart and soul.

.

*January 28*

## FORM AND FORMLESS

With certainty look upon the face of another and know that you are seeing the face of God. With certainty, look into a mirror and see the same. Ah, but there enters the doubt. "How can this be God?" you ask, and this is where you lack in understanding. Allow us to help.

You are seeing one aspect of a multi-faceted jewel. You are seeing the form of that which is both form and formless. You are both form and formless. Your friend is both form and formless, and all of it—the form and formless—is God. Would you shut out any of it for the false belief that only the formless is God? It is all God, and it is you, your friend, and all that is.

Celebrate your Divinity today. It is all Love. Anything that is not love is merely the lack of understanding of all that we have shared with you today. Be the Presence of Love today and fulfill your purpose in Life.

## A NEW WAY OF SEEING

In every man's heart there is goodness. Do not forget this. It is easy to believe this is a lie when you see a man or woman performing acts contrary to what you know as goodness. But always remember that beyond the body, beyond appearances, lies the Soul, which is naught but good, naught but God, or that being you perceive would not be there for you to perceive.

See beyond perceived "badness" and look for the Good. If it is occluded from your sight, ask your soul why this is so. Is it the fault of the other or of your own perception, or of both? Are you truly separate? If you believe the answer to be yes, then you will continue to see "badness." If you know the answer to be no, then you will see the "goodness" even if your fellow humans would judge differently.

Open your heart and you will open your eyes to a new way of seeing.

# January 30

## ABOVE THE PETTINESS

Rise above the pettiness. Rise above it all. Do not allow yourself to be dragged down. For this you are given free will. It is your choice. Do you succumb, and become irritable, and lash out, or do you go within and find peace?

Peace is always waiting. It is a state of consciousness you know quite well as spirit, but in physical form you oft forget. Whatever tricks you need to employ to tell the ego to get out of the way, employ them. Beyond the physical world with its ups and downs and instant changes from good mood to bad lies a state where nothing changes. It is the state of simply being ... the state of pure consciousness which simply IS and simply knows naught but love. How could such a state have ups and downs? How could it be anything but peace?

When your state of consciousness rises and falls like a wave, go within to the deepest part of the ocean of which you are a part, and there find peace.

## YOU ARE THE WAY AND THE LIGHT

Joy to the world. That is what we wish you to bring: joy, love, and hope. "Oh, but I am just one person!" you cry, and in one sense this is true. In the greater sense, you are All That Is. What if all humans felt they could make no difference?

Keep chipping away at the darkness. Be the light that shines ever brighter, bringing love where there is anger and hatred. How refreshing!

Joy to the world, the Lord is come to this earth in the form of you! Quite a responsibility it is, but you are up to the task. Each and every one of you awakened souls brings a beacon of light in a sea of darkness.

Go forth today and be a messenger. Hold your lantern high as you shine it upon those whose eyes are closed. At first they will balk and shade the eyes. Faced with such darkness, however, they will come around one by one. It may seem a daunting task, but this is the way, and you are it.

## *February 1*

### RAISING THE SPIRITS

Do you think those on the other side have no sense of humor? Quite the contrary. We are quite aware of the healing effects of laughter.

There is no better way to raise the spirits than to enjoy some fun. That is what life is all about—raising the spirits. To make another laugh is to bring about a heart connection. There is a great connection between love and laughter. Of course we do not speak of laughter at the expense of another, but laughter for the pure joy that comes from seeing the humor in life's adventures.

Do not take life so seriously. Raise the roof with laughter and raise the world's vibration in doing so.

## THE POWER OF LOVE

A baby takes its first breath and cries.
Such a shock to have left the womb.
What is it that calms the distress?
A caress.
Once held to the breast,
The crying decreases.
Or ceases.
This is the power of love.
From love you came, to love you will return.
For now, you learn.
This is life, full of first breaths,
Full of lessons that cause you to cry.
And then you die.
But life goes on.  Death is not the end.
Merely the last breath of this book.
But look!
Now you can truly breathe.
You are given a reprieve.
A new state awaits where love surrounds ...
In fact, abounds.
A time of rest, a time of peace
Before you cry anew.
This is you.

*February 3*

## CHOICES YET AGAIN

It is fear that keeps you stuck. You are unhappy in a situation yet you are comfortable there. You would rather remain unhappy than to make choices which will undoubtedly create change. Do you not know that all in the human life changes constantly? You can sit back clinging to the illusion of security or create a far greater security by taking charge of creating your future.

If you are unhappy, there is a reason for this. Your unhappiness is a sign that better choices can be made. It is your choices which have created your situation. Ah. Now you balk. And now you blame your situation on others. There is only one Mind, one Consciousness interacting with Itself. You control what is projected onto your screen. Will you remain unhappy, or will you make choices, asking for guidance, if you will, and create a more peaceful "now"?

## WITHOUT WORDS

"There are no words to say ..." that is because words are so very limiting. One culture has 26 words for a concept, yet another has one. In one culture the tone of voice changes the meaning of a word. You experience a variety of emotions that cover a limitless scale, yet you attempt to put a word to each one. How many shades of red are there? How many shades of blue? How many shades of love exist?

Do us a favor. Look into the eyes of a loved one and feel the love, but do not put words to the experience. Look at a beautiful scene in nature today, but deliberately delete the thought-words. Omit verbal experience on purpose. Simply feel it in its many shades, its many nuances. In doing so, you have come a bit closer to your true nature and to the world which awaits you in all of its fullness.

You can spend a day in silence and still have thoughts that pass through your brain in the form of words. This defeats the point we make today. Silence even the thoughts and return to the most basic part of existence. Experience this aspect of yourself and take a step toward infinity.

*February 5*

## SWEETENER

Love is the syrup on the pancakes, the icing on the cake. Silly analogies, but what are words, but literary paints. Allow us to dip our brush in the pot of paint and color in your world with words descriptive enough to change your way of thinking.

See the world anew in each moment. Why do you have this? Why do you do that? Why do you put syrup on your pancakes? To add sweetness, to take a good thing and make it even more enjoyable.

You can add love to anything and make it more palatable, more enjoyable. Slather it on thickly or simply drizzle it in droplets. Play with it like your finger paints, and have fun with what you create.

Paint your world, sweeten your world with colors, with words, with thoughts, using the greatest medium of creation ... love ... and then watch your world take on new levels of meaning, harmony, and sweetness.

## THAT VITAL FLOW

A pin pricks the finger and it bleeds. Just a drop comes out and you stare at it. The dot of bright, red color is in such contrast to the skin. "Is that really inside of me?" It is so easy to forget that this vital fluid flows constantly through the body or the body would cease to exist.

There is another vital flow within you and around you. It is the Life Force. Were it not for this Force flowing through you, the body would cease to exist. It is in such great contrast to the body that were you able to see it, you would stare, transfixed, just as you do at a drop of blood.

You cannot see Spirit, but you can feel it. Sit quietly and take a few deep breaths. Concentrate on one word only to quiet the mind: "Love." Sit there as long as it takes ... as many days in a row as it takes ... and when you finally feel the Presence of that word that you are repeating, then you need not see the spirit ever, for you will truly know that it flows through you. You need not prick the finger to let it flow outside of you, for it is all of you.

May your spirit bleed through all that you do, leaving an indelible mark on all you touch.

*February 7*

## SO IT IS

You may not hear from friends or family every day, but this does not mean they do not hold you in their thoughts. You may go a while without thinking of another, but this does not mean you have not been connected. Once connected, you are always linked at the subconscious level.

A strong prayer issued on one's behalf remains in effect, for you have set it in motion. It gathers energy when joined by the prayers of others. You may add fuel to this creation as you wish, but there is no need to do so constantly. We say again, once created, so it is. See it as such, and know that prayers are answered.

You are all interconnected, for there is only one Consciousness. It may appear that you are having separate experiences, so enjoy them. Meanwhile, know that your friends and family are with you and you with them. In reality, there is no separation.

.

## THE "I" IN THE CENTER

How do you find peace in the midst of a storm? You go to the eye—
the center—which is always there. When caught in the worst of the
winds it may be a struggle to find your way to the center, but trust that
it is there.

Relax the body. Take the mind off the thoughts. Breathe deeply and
set your intention on reaching that place of calmness. When you reach
it, relax even more, and then pray. It is here, in the silence, that you
will hear guidance—the lifesavers sent out to you.

You can call out at any time, but in the calm eye you connect clearly
with the greater "I" of the Self and remember that the storm is always
temporary. This too shall pass, but the peace that passes all
understanding is always there.

## STILL RIGHT HERE

Broken hearts mend slowly.
It takes time to heal a wound.
When what was had you now have lost,
By grief you are consumed.

See not the shell that's left behind
When one you lost has now departed.
Focus on the love you shared
The high vibrations that you started.

This energy stays with you
Even though the person stands no more.
And no longer can you see them
When they pass through Heaven's door.

The grief will lift, the heart will mend,
But always will you miss them,
For you focus on the things you've lost ...
The fact that you can't kiss them.

They're here, we say, held safe and sound.
So speak their name aloud.
And know that they are by your side,
Not floating on some cloud.

For spirit are you here and now
As is the one who left.
Not lost, not gone, but with you still,
With no need to be bereft.

## A BALANCED LIFE

You walk a tightrope between the physical and spirit world. It is a balancing act. Where you do you place your focus? You place your attention on this physical life, for that is why you are here—to learn from it and from the others around you ... all of you beautiful souls emerging at different rates into the light. But whilst you are in this world, you maintain the balance simply by keeping in mind as often as possible that you are in this world but not of it. You are a spirit-being first and foremost.

What does this recollection do for you? It reminds you to pay attention to your thoughts, to be the presence of Love, and to give gratitude to God for this life. These are things you can do at any moment and at all moments whilst walking about in your human suit. When you remember to keep this balance in your life, your life flows ever more smoothly. Say your prayers, sit in meditation, do a bit of spiritual reading, and attune to higher consciousness on a regular basis, and you will have a balanced life.

*February 11*

## IMAGINARY DRAGONS

Be not afraid on this new leg of your journey. Be not afraid ever, whatever leg of this eternal existence you embark upon. Of what is there to be afraid? There be no dragons. These exist only in the mind. "No, I see them!" you cry. "They are all around me!" Then slay them with your mind as well. When you understand that the only reality is Spirit, which is pure consciousness, then you create and destroy your demons with the same.

Nothing can harm the real you. Such power comes with this awareness! Imaginary dragons may snap at your imaginary feet, and you can laugh or cry. It is your choice. Inside it is always peaceful, always now. When faced with perceived turmoil, return inside to the ever-present peace and smile.

## PERFECT RIGHT NOW

You have all that you need as a spiritual being in this very moment. This is not something you obtain. You are that perfect spirit now. It is, however, something which you awaken to, or you may understand it as "returning to."

You are and always have been perfect, unlimited, and connected with All That Is. You did agree, however, to be denied the full awareness of your true nature so that you could make choices as a human being. The very process of making choices removes the mask and reveals the spirit bit by bit.

A choice in one direction leaves the mask in place. A choice in another direction reveals more of the perfection that is already there. This choice can be as simple as, "Do I respond with love or with angry words?" It is not so simple for the human, perhaps, but when you make it your life's quest to reveal the perfection that is you, the way is revealed far more often.

*February 13*

## THE REAL DEAL

What does it mean when something is genuine? It is the real deal, not a fake or an imposter. You like genuine things. They represent value, solidity, trust, and longevity.

Spirit is genuine. It is made of love, the greatest thing of value that exists. Ego is not genuine. Have you not heard people exclaim, "Oh, he or she is so fake!" Spirit knows when one is coming from love, aligned with the spirit aspect, or coming from ego.

Be genuine in your thoughts and actions today and every day. It feels good to you and to others, for only love is real. Only love is lasting. It is the real deal.

## LOVE WITHOUT CONDITIONS

What conditions are you placing on your loved ones? Love unconditionally. Why should you? It is simple: because love is all you are. Call it Spirit ... call it Consciousness ... call it God ... it is all the same energy. Love is the highest vibration of this energy. This is your Source. The higher you raise your personal vibration, the closer you become to your Source and reveal your true nature.

When you place conditions upon the love you feel toward others, you are constricting the flow—constricting your Self. How many times a day do you look at one whom you claim to love and think, "He or she should not do this or that." "He or she should not think that way or speak that way or act that way." Who are you to say how another should behave or think? Each is on his own path. It is best to concern yourself with your own soul's development.

One of the fastest ways in which you can develop is by ceasing judgment of others, especially those most close to you—your greatest teachers—and sending them only love ... loving without conditions. When you can master this key step—to love all beings without condition—then you will live as The Master ... a most lofty goal, but one well within your reach. Examine your thoughts. Do you truly love others, or just parts of others? True love encompasses all parts without condition.

## A THOUGHT AWAY

Distance does not separate us.
We're not so far away.
Take in a breath and blow it out.
Say what you want to say.

We hear you as you sit and breathe
And contemplate the light,
For deep inside is where we live
Not far away and out of sight.

Our world is yours; it's not distinct,
Just varying vibrations,
Not divided by false borders
Like geographic nations.

To join the two just close your eyes
And loving thoughts bring to your mind,
And there our worlds meet on the breath
Like two hearts intertwined.

A thought away, that's all we are,
So keep us close at hand.
For now you cannot touch us
But at your side is where we stand.

## EXPECTATIONS

Skeptics as a whole are a bit of a negative bunch, are they not? Mind you, it is good to be wary at times when dealing with those who are more human-oriented than spirit-oriented, but there is a difference between being wary and being close-minded. When you say to yourself, "This is probably not going to happen," you set up a frequency in your field that virtually guarantees you will achieve the result you expect.

Think of those you know who always see the glass as half empty. And so it is. Consciousness creates reality. It can be no other way. Have you achieved the goals, the life, the reality you desire? How do you see the glass? Do not take this expression for granted. Examine it. You have a glass with liquid to the half-way mark. Do you say, "Oh, woe is me! It is already half gone!" or do you say, "Oh, look at that! There is still half left!" Each carries quite a different vibration. What created that vibration that was felt in you as an emotion? Consciousness, plain and simple. You create your emotions with your consciousness. You also create your external reality.

The glass with the liquid at the halfway point is completely neutral. How do you wish to feel today: empty or full-filled? Even if your cup has love at the halfway point, recognize it as such and it will fill the rest of the way by way of your choosing.

Yes, you do indeed create your own reality, to the point of cancelling out others' efforts in the physical world, even when they might serve your own interests. Do you see how very powerful and how very important are your thoughts?

## February 17

### A REASON TO PRAY

Yes, celebrate the successes: The operation went well. The talk was well received. The family visit passed without incident. You arrived safely at your destination. The prayers worked well. Now you can relax. Yes, relax, but do not stop praying. We say this not to indicate that once again you need worry. We say it as a reminder that the prayers kept you in a state of communion with Higher Consciousness. Why should you go to this state only when you need a favor?

In a world of duality such as you inhabit whilst in human form, there will always be ups and downs. That is the nature of your reality. Do not pray only for the good times and only in the bad times. Pray ceaselessly prayers of gratitude for the very communion you enjoy whilst in prayer. It is this communion which sustains you. Sustain the connection, and there you will find the strength, courage, and peace of mind to travel well from moment to moment.

## OPENING THE CONNECTION

Life can seem cold and hard at times. This is what happens when the heart is shut off. Do you know that you control this connection? That is what the heart is – a connection point between you and all else. You open and shut this connection with the mind, oft times unconsciously.

Are you feeling cut off, alone, cold, separate? Sit quietly and picture someone or something such as a kitten or a puppy that makes your heart sing. Imagine holding that person or creature to your heart. You will feel this area open as you open the connection. Now that you remember how this feels, maintain the connection. Holding it open, think of someone else and send that energy outward toward them.

It is all a mental exercise, yet very real. You are never alone. You are never cut off, save in your own mind. Use that very mind to bring yourself back into alignment with your true self and with All That Is.

*February 19*

## ON THE FRINGES

On the fringes. Is that where you are?

What are fringes, but dangling pieces that hang from the main body of a piece of cloth. Picture the mass consciousness as the cloth, and those who dare to think differently as the fringes. Is this so bad?

It is the mass belief in a judgmental God that keeps man judging man. It is the mass belief that you are all separate that makes it difficult for one man to forgive another.

Remain on the fringes if you can, sending your higher vibrations ever upward from where you hang and change the very fabric of your world.

## WITH PEACE IN YOUR HEART

You pass a beggar on the street. He holds out a hand and you cringe. What goes through your head? Is it contempt or is it compassion? He is learning lessons, and so are you. If you give him money, do you help or hinder him? If you withhold your coins, do you help or hinder yourself? The difference is not in the coins you give, but in what is in your heart.

The beggar will learn lessons whether you give money or not. He will appreciate you or not. You perhaps may not be able to give coins to every beggar, but there is one gift you can give: a prayer filled with love and thanks that all will grow whilst here ... that all may see the perfection in each being's present circumstances as a path toward that growth ...that all will see a brighter light and move inexorably toward it ... that all will know how very much they are loved ... that all—including you—will find peace in your heart.

Without peace, all are beggars.

*February 21*

## ROOMS

How do you remain calm in the face of death? It is easy when you know the Truth that death is merely a door to the next room. Do you fear walking from one room to another here in your reality? The furnishings may change, as may the colors on the walls, but you did not change as you stepped across the threshold. Thus, you had no fear. It is the same when the spirit leaves the body. The colors you perceive may be more brilliant, the "furnishings" may sparkle a bit more, but you did not change at all. The real you remained as pure consciousness and love at the core.

Some fear death, fearing nothing but darkness. What do you do when you step into a darkened room in your house? You turn on the lights and lo! You discover the room is filled with things to behold, awaiting your experiences there.

Your Father's mansion has many rooms. To turn on the lights, you need merely flip the switch. That switch lies within you. It is operated by your consciousness as spirit, not as a human in physical form. Do not fear death for yourself or others. Know that your entire existence consists of stepping eternally from one room to another and turning on the lights.

GOING HOME

Do not fear death. It comes to all. You merely fear the unknown and the perceived pain of those you will leave behind. All of life in physical form is a preparation for the next step. Death is merely taking that step back to the realm of love from which you came ... your true home. You cling to this one for it is all you currently know with your focus so firmly rooted here.

Think of life before having children. You think there can be no greater love than that which you know, until along comes a child, and then you know unconditional love. You are as the childless one now. Death re-introduces you to a far greater form of unconditional love than you can presently imagine.

Have no fear. The grieving process is one all must face. Suffer not from fear. Live fully now and simply allow life to flow. Rest in peace here and now, my child, for death is merely a transition home. Life continues eternally. Find the peace in knowing this and bring the love to this experience now.

*February 23*

## THE ONLY THING THAT MATTERS

You have all now that you will ever need. We are speaking in terms of the non-physical, for in the physical world you look about you and see things. How many things do you need? Is that truly what you need? What do they bring you? Satisfaction? Joy? Happiness? In some cases, yes, but where does it end, this desire for things?

Enjoy your things. Acquire without guilt, but never forget that it is not the thing itself which brings you joy, but your perception of its value to you. With this perception comes emotion. That is the thing you desire—not the thing itself, but how the thing makes you feel. Beware of this, for nothing but your own thoughts about a thing make you feel anything at all.

You are more than your thoughts and emotions. You are far more than any thing. You are Life itself ...spirit without form. As spirit you need no thing. Love is not a thing. It does not come in a bottle or a bauble. It is already inside you, bottled up until you release it. You have all that you need at this very moment, and every moment that is, for Love IS.

Love is, and you are that. Let no thing come between you and your realization of that.

## ONLY FOR AWHILE

Saying goodbye is never easy when the one who is leaving is dear to the heart. You miss one near to you in proportion to how much you love. Celebrate your grief. It is a sign that you have loved fully. Yes, it is painful. Of course you do not want to feel it, but would you have missed out on the joy as well? Feel the pain, but do not hold onto it. Wash it through you with your tears at the rate that is right for you. Then you can get back to the love, which will always be there.

Your loved one is going away for a while, as will you some day, and then you will be reunited. No separation is forever, for there is no such thing as forever, only spaces in between in which to know the full depth of feeling.

Celebrate the ups and downs, for they are all part of life. It does go on, allowing you to love and love again. You will see each other again, for love does not die. It is just a temporary goodbye.

*February 25*

## THE WEB

You see a frown and bristle.
Your anger flares as well.
If you were in the other's mind,
Oh, what a tale their thoughts would tell.

All that you see's not as you think
Yet instantly you fear
That others will cause threat and harm
To what you hold most dear.

Be not concerned with others' acts
Their thoughts or 'ere their deeds.
Just focus on <u>your</u> inner thoughts
On your individual needs.

Each one is caught in his own web
And seldom understands
That each is well connected
By Spirit's glistening strands.

Pay attention to your inner world
And what you radiate
For what you send into the web
Is what will be your fate.

## ALL THAT IS

"All That Is." How often do you hear this term for your Source? Do you take it literally, or do you envision exclusions? Does the All That Is include the terrorist? Does the All That Is include the so-called sinner?

Within all things is a Spark, or that thing or being would not exist. In some the light is so clouded you cannot see it, but Spirit is omnipresent. "All That Is" means exactly that. It means you, as well. You are a facet of All That Is just as Jesus, Krishna, Buddha, and Muhammad were and are facets of All That Is.

All merely display greater or lesser light. There are no exclusions. See yourself as part of That and realize how very vital is your role. See how you fit in with That and That and That and feel your connection. You do not stand alone, and you cannot fall. Rise above your human consciousness.

See the world with spiritual consciousness, for that is All That Is.

*February 27*

## THIS LIVING METAPHOR

Glorious weather brings a smile to your lips. You raise your eyes to the sky and bask in the warm sunshine. Why this upliftment? Why do you not feel the same when the sky is gray and cloudy? All of life is a metaphor. All is simply a different way of expressing the same thing: God.

God is light, and warmth, and goodness. How do you define these? You use words and images to describe the indescribable. God is a feeling. That God exists at all is a knowingness within the heart. Even this heart is a metaphor, is it not? Clouds obscure the light. These clouds are like your thoughts, which obscure the Light within your heart. Is it any wonder you long for the sun to come out and warm you with its rays?

Raise your face to the sky and give thanks, not only for the sun, but for the clouds as well. All you see and all you experience is evidence of God. The clouds exist to bring you closer to the light, for how would you recognize the light if you did not know darkness?

Rejoice in every moment of this living metaphor you call Life.

## CHANGE IS A'COMIN'

Center yourself, then get out of the way. You, as the ego, are your own worst foe when it comes to advancing. You cling so very tightly to established ways of thinking and doing. It is these very habits which hold you back.

You must be open to change if you are to grow. What does growth imply? Change. What is stagnation? Staying the same. You abhor change, yet you desire growth. Do you see the irony? Make yourself vulnerable. Welcome change. Invite growth—spiritual growth.

Yes, your life will change. It will change for the better, but you cannot see this with your spiritual eyes closed. Close your physical eyes and pray, "Thank you for this awakening. I am ready to grow. I welcome change." Then, sit back and buckle your seat belt.

*March 1*

## COMING OUT

Oh, how you lie to each other. You go out in public and put a smile on your face as if nothing is wrong. You hide behind that mask, for that is what you have been taught to do. Inside your heart is breaking. Inside is great turmoil, yet that is where you keep it.

Do you not know that you and another you encounter may be encountering the self-same challenges? You think you must put up a brave front and face your challenges alone. From whence comes this silly notion that you must be perfect and perfectly happy?

Yes, all is in perfect order always. Yes, you create your own happiness with your thoughts, but we advise you to ask for assistance. Have we not told you that you are never alone? You have unseen helpers, but we send you many helpers in the physical world as well. Let down your guard a bit and allow your helpers to ask, "Is there something wrong? How may I help?"

Life is full of challenges. They come so that you will learn to make choices in favor of love. This begins with loving yourself enough to not hide behind a mask.

## ALWAYS, ALWAYS, ALWAYS

"Where have you been?" you ask when you have gone through a drought of not feeling the connection, and we remind you that we are always here.

There are a variety of reasons you may not feel the presence of your unseen helpers. The physical body and its ailments can be a distraction as can your mind. Are you preoccupied with earthly thoughts? These push away celestial awareness.

Clear the mind and clear the body of so-called "junk" and then you will find us--always waiting in the wings, always watching, and always here for the asking. Relax. You do not have to go it alone.

*March 3*

MOVING ON

When you cannot forgive the self, step above and see yourself as we do. It is not necessary to continue berating the self. Once the mistake has been recognized and adjusted, it is time to move on. Cease reliving it. This serves no purpose.

If you must obsess about something, then ceaselessly see yourself now modeling the behavior you know is best. See yourself acting as the spirit-being you know yourself to be. From this higher perspective, see all of your fellow human beings struggling, including yourself. They forgive you when you are contrite. Let go of the weight with gratitude for the lesson learned and move on.

Get your feet out of the mud. Clean them off and leave no dirty footprints.

## SEEING BEYOND THE ACTIONS

"I forgive you" … three of the most healing words you can say and hear. They say to another, "I recognize that beneath the action which I perceived as hurtful there lies a being just like me. We may never see things the same. We may never act the same, but at the very core we are the same. When we take away all thought and all actions, we are love, for we both come from the Source of all love."

When one says, "I forgive you," one is saying, "I see past your humanity, for I am human, too. I know what lies beneath that humanity, for it lies within me, too. In forgiving you, I help the spirit being within me to rise and emerge. May my forgiveness help you to recognize that same spirit within you."

When all can see the Spirit within each other, there will be no more need for forgiveness.

*March 5*

## THE GREATEST GIFT

You package your gifts in a box, then wrap them in colorful paper. Why do you do this? So that the recipient does not know in advance what treasure lies inside.

You are gift-wrapped, my friend. God has packaged you for a while in the most beautiful of wrappings: a human body. Each of you is decorated just a bit differently from the other, but the treasure inside all holds the same essence of its Giver.

It is your task in life to open the package and behold the gift that lies there hidden. Will you be one of those careful beings who removes the wrapping oh so very carefully, peeling away each corner and very slowly revealing the contents to yourself and others? Or will you rip off the wrapping with utter abandonment and joy? Both methods are fine. Worry not, as long as you savor the process. Ultimately, the treasure is revealed to all.

LET IT BLOOM


Pick a flower from your garden.
Put it in a vase.
To smell its fragrance and see it there
Brings a smile to your face.

A flower is a symbol,
A thing of beauty to behold,
A sign that love is everywhere
A story to be told.

Look around you daily.
See the signs of love in all
In the beauty of a flower
In the cry of a bird's call.

Yes, stop and smell the roses
Smell their sweet perfume.
Bring this beauty to your heart
And feel the love inside you bloom.

You are a part of all that is.
You are the beauty in a flower.
You are the majesty of all you see
For you carry in you God's great power.

That power is the love you feel
Each time you stop and pause
It's then you know that all you see
Is the effect of one great Cause.

*March 7*

## PART OF A TEAM

Celebrate your successes, but be mindful of how they came about. Did you act as a lone agent, or part of a team? Are you really able to do anything by yourself?

It is impossible to act alone, for you are intimately interconnected with All That Is. You breathe and you take credit for this. Can you stop the passage of the soul from life in physical form to spirit form? Your doctors attempt to do this, and you call it "playing God."

So, you see, at some level you do know that all that you do—from breathing to simply being—happens as part of a team: the "little i" and the "Big I". Go ahead and take credit when you do well, but take a moment and give credit where it is due: to that greater part of You.

## WITH FERVOR

Every time you sit to pray, you acknowledge that there is something greater than yourself. What is it that you pray for? Instead of asking, we advise you to give thanks for these things as if they are already your reality.

All exists. God exists. God is, indeed, all goodness and all love. If that for which you pray adds to the goodness and love of the whole, why would you need to ask for it at all? You need only give thanks for God's will being done through you.

There is only One Mind. Would not, then, that Mind know not only every hair on your head but your every desire? The truth is, you need not pray at all, but it is the most effective way of reminding the human side of you that you are Spirit. It reconnects you with your Source and allows that Divine energy to flow more freely.

So, yes, pray fervently … prayers of gratitude for your awakening to these truths.

*March 9*

## THE PRESENT

The part of you that is spirit only knows one tense: the present tense. The part of you that is ego knows two others: past and future. This constant drifting in and out of past tense and future tense keeps the body tense, and ego enjoys this game.

Tension maintains separation and maintains ego's perceived power over spirit. Peace allows you to know oneness. Peace is found in the present. Remaining present takes awareness of the thoughts. Thoughts bounce from past to present to future to past to future to present and so on like a ping pong ball out of control. Back and forth you go, from worry to pain with moments of equanimity in between, but just enough uncertainty for ego to run rampant.

"Be here now" – excellent advice for finding peace. Grab the ping pong ball and plant it firmly in your lap for a few moments each hour. Breathe deeply and simply sit with your focus on your breath or on a peaceful phrase. "What good does that do?" you ask. Quite a bit, you will find, if you try it. For just a few moments you are present. No worry. No fear of the future. No pain from painful memories of the past. You are simply watching the breath like soft clouds that float past, and in that moment you are free of ego's grip—a free spirit—and that is the present all can enjoy.

## MAN'S BEST FRIEND

The seeing eye dog … man's best friend with an important role: to act as the physical eyes of one who cannot see, to warn of dangers, and protect its master. While there is a master-servant relationship, do you not see that the two are also bonded by love?

You have within you a Seeing Eye. It guides you through the darkness when you know not which way to turn. It keeps you out of trouble, nudging you ever so gently and at times a bit forcefully, urging you to act when you are in danger. This Seeing Eye is a source of unconditional love that goes with you everywhere. How often do you praise it, thank it, give it strokes, and acknowledgment?

It will remain at your side through thick and thin, asking little in return, but a little acknowledgment and gratitude are quite appreciated. Were it not for this Seeing Eye, you would stumble far more often. Be not blind to your helper—this connection to the one who guards the light within. Spend time getting to know it. We daresay it will become your greatest, most trusted companion.

*March 11*

## STICKY FINGERS

Pickpockets—thieves who reach into your purse or pockets and steal your belongings without you even realizing it. So clever are they. So quick and nimble that you do not even know that you have been robbed until you discover that your valuables are gone.

Do you not realize that you are surrounded by spiritual pickpockets? Unlike the actual thieves, many of these do not rob you deliberately. They get into your energy field and with a thought or word deplete your own energy. The funny thing is, you allow this. You may sense danger, but you allow them near. You know who the thieves are. You share space with some of them quite often. They will steal you blind if you let them.

First, you must become conscious that your spiritual pockets are being picked. What is your greatest defense? Awareness. It is not your task to fight them off. This can be harmful to you. Your greatest weapon is always love. Cancel out the sticky fingers of negativity with loving energy in the form of your own loving choices and thoughts.

Others' energy can harm you if you remain unaware of their energy. Be vigilant and surround yourself not with a barrier, but with rays of love. Fill your pockets with love. In this way, when the thieves dip inside your field, they will either be changed or take their business elsewhere.

Each is on his own path. May your pockets and your path be lined with love.

## TAKE A DEEP BREATH

Yes, it is all about love. Can you ever hear this message enough? Not enough or too much, for it is the most important message in the Universe—to love thy brother as thyself and love Spirit with all thy heart and soul. The problem comes when you do not love yourself enough. Then it becomes impossible to love your fellow human beings. Then you act in ways contrary to your nature, either out of fear or to get love through manipulations instead of merely expressing your innate spirit nature.

Take a deep breath. Focus on your heart, and repeat after us: "I am loved." Now, carry that feeling with you today, unless you do not believe the words to be true. If that is the case, remain where you are and ask for Grace to show you the Truth. You already know it in your heart. Now believe it.

*March 13*

## THE KEYS OF CREATION

Can you see into the future? Then it already exists.

What you see in your mind becomes reality when you see it clearly, feel it as an accomplished event, and it serves the greater good. Ah yes, there's the rub. You are a co-creator, not the sole creator. Other factors come into play. This is a bit of a safety measure—a sort of "for your own good" clause the Universe leaves in place for those of you with free will.

Create your future as best you can. See it, feel it, and then ask that the greatest good surround your vision and make it what you need best to grow. Oft times your view is limited, and so you have a bit of help.

Clear vision accompanied by strong emotion and a desire that the greatest good be served—these are the keys of creation.

## NOTHING LESS

At times you do need protection. At times negativity surrounds you. This is life in your reality. All are at different stages of their soul's evolution. You must make choices from moment to moment. Do you wish to grow, stay the same, or allow yourself to slip back?

Growth is measured in your capacity to express love. As you grow, your consciousness rises. You give off higher vibrations. Others around you may not.

Visualize a shield of protective energy around you when surrounded by less than pure light. May this shield be semi-permeable so that only the highest rays get in and all of your rays flow outward. Does this seem silly to you? You are pure energy. All solidity is an illusion. You work with energy using your consciousness. As you become conscious of this truth, the more you are able to fulfill your purpose of being the presence of Love, the highest vibration.

*March 15*

PERSPECTIVE

Relax. It is all perfect. "But my life is far from perfect!" you protest. We ask you to look back upon your greatest challenges. Perhaps they did not seem perfect at the time, but did you not grow from them? Are you not stronger now? Did you not learn?

Life is orderly, not chaotic. Yes, there is seeming chaos at times, but even at those times there is order. You must look back in time to see the perfection and the order, for at this time you have a limited perspective.

There will come a time when you can see the greater perspective at once. Until that time, relax and trust. Worry does no good. Anxiety serves you not. Trust brings you peace.

Peace be upon you as you trust that all is in perfect order always.

## SPIRITED

What if you truly were only human and not a spirit-being in human form? What if Spirit did not guide you? Why, then you would all be like the robots you see in your science fiction movies: mechanistic beings devoid of emotion. You would go about your business interacting and carrying out your functions. When one robot ceased functioning due to an irreparable malfunction, you would place it in the recycle bin and be done with it. End of story.

But instead, you love. Because of this, you have elaborate ceremonies when the body no longer functions and yes, you grieve. You feel loss because you love. You grieve because you are not a robot; you have a heart. You have a human heart that pumps blood through the body in robotic, mechanistic function, but you have an emotional heart, for you are spirit, and love is your very essence.

Spirit is recycled, for life is eternal. Love is never-ending. Grief and loss turn into rebirth and rejoicing. Rejoice that you feel your emotions. Appreciate all of them. Were it not for the joy and the pain, there would be no life.

*March 17*

## FOR ONE WHOLE DAY

Put your worries in a box and put a lid on them. Close the lid tightly. Trust us, they will squawk a bit, but do not re-open the box, no matter how uncomfortable you are without them. They will be fine in there all together, for worries thrive on each other.

What will you do now that you are worry free? First of all, buy yourself some heavier shoes, for you will want to float free of the ground without that extra weight. Next, prepare your explanation, for everyone will want to know why you look so carefree.

At the end of the day, take your worries out of the box and put them back in place. What? You no longer wish to carry them around after a day of freedom? All right, then. Leave them in the box. It is your choice. It has always been your choice. Now go get a good night's rest, knowing you never really needed those worries anyway. You have gotten along quite well without them, and the world went on.

## AMAZING

You are amazing … just the way you are. Yes, these are lyrics to a song, but they bear repeating for all who read these words. You sing your songs over and over, but do you tell yourself the words you most often need to hear over and over? Not enough, my friend.

You are amazing … an amazing child of God. Do not worry so much about self-improvement. Sit back, look in a mirror and see the amazing things we see in you. See through the eyes of God, not the ego who cringes at the mere thought of looking in a mirror.

Your every cell is amazing. Your body is amazing. Your mind is amazing. Your spirit is amazing. Why are you so critical? That is learned behavior. Do us a favor: Learn to see yourself the way we do.

You are amazing … just the way you are.

*March 19*

EFFORTLESS

Some of your greatest discoveries have come when you stopped trying.

Release the effort. Unclench the mind and drift. In this way you connect with genius. In this way you allow creativity to flow. You cannot find your keys? Stop searching and allow them to come to you.

It is the human who needs to work at things, to struggle ... or so you think. Realize that you have a direct connection to your Source with many helpers along the conduit. Let them do the searching for you. They will provide all of the creativity you need. For now, plant the seed of that which you wish to create or find, then sit back and watch it grow.

## REFLECTING

If you were to shatter a mirror, would any of the pieces be any less reflective than before? Not at all. Each would retain its original quality. You are a shard of the Mirror of which you are made—no less magnificent for your size.

Do not take the physical into consideration when thinking about your true nature, for physicality has nothing to do with the part of you that is essential. Breathe in deeply and follow the breath inward, inward, inward. Now exhale and follow the breath outward, outward, outward endlessly. There. You have just had the tiniest inkling of who you are. Your breath merges with that of all others and all that is.

For now you are merely enjoying an experience of the in and out-breathing of the Great Soul. May your loving actions today be the perfect reflection of who you really are.

*March 21*

## THE PURPOSE OF PAIN

"Why do I repeat the same mistakes again and again? It is like banging my head against a wall." Again, it comes back to the difference between ego and spirit. You are both of these at once. It is merely a matter of which aspect of the self you are allowing to take precedence.

When you hit a wall repeatedly or encounter difficulties, this is a sign that you are out of alignment with your spirit. The lessons will continue to be attention-getting in a painful way until you recognize this. Pain serves a purpose. Were there no pain, you would not learn. Some people have a greater tolerance for pain, and thus take a while longer to learn. Others need merely a slight prick of the finger to open the eyes and say, "I remember (that I am spirit)! I surrender my (ego's) need to do and have things the way I (as ego) think they should be. Now please guide me to a healthier, safer way of being."

As you surrender and align with Spirit, your life will flow. Things will fall into place painlessly. If you still feel emotional pain as a result of your choices, please examine your thoughts, for this could be ego resisting changes that are in your best interest.

Always, always let the heart be your guide. It speaks Truth, even if you do not always want to hear it.

## NOT SO SERIOUS

Fun is the word of the day. Can you relax and let down a bit? It is not necessary to take this life and its many experiences so seriously. Do you not enjoy playing? Do you not enjoy a bit of fun? Can you not see how the Mind that created this dream in which you are a part would far rather have a bit of fun than a melodrama?

This dream on the cosmic scale has already played out. So if you can relax and enjoy yourself, you will have a far easier go of it. Some of you will bristle at this suggestion, for you are mired in misery. Know that part of this life experience is playing, experimenting with how you choose to react to life events.

We do not wish to downplay your challenges, but begin now and bit by bit try to see your life as play. Insert fun wherever and whenever you can. All is temporary. All will pass. Do not take any of it too seriously. Smile more often.

Yet another recipe for peace.

*March 23*

## PART OF THE WHOLE

You become discouraged when you see how many people exist and how few of them seem to think as you do, love as you do. Is it all in vain, you wonder? And now we ask you to think of the human body yet again as an example. Trillions of cells run around in the body, some bumping into each other, others never meeting, yet each of them playing a role. Yes, the body could live without you, but you exist for a reason: to add to the whole.

As above, so below. Do not concern yourself with the health of every other cell. There is one Consciousness overseeing all of that. Concern yourself with your own health, your spiritual, mental, emotional, and physical health. May it be as strong as possible, as balanced as possible. In so doing, you bring health to the whole in your own way.

You may not feel the effects of this now, but do not concern yourself with this. There is a reason that you care whilst others may not. Simply trust and soldier on.

All is well as long as you "are", and trust this as well: You will always "be."

## NEW PERSPECTIVE

Prepare yourself. There will be quite a surprise when you finally wake up. You will find that many of the things you held dear are actually not so important, and those things you may have pushed to the side are more important. In actuality, nothing is more or less of anything. Everything simply IS, and it is in enjoying the existence of all that is that you grow.

Life is for the experience of it. Nothing more. If you can bring more peace, joy, and love to the experience while you have it, the experience will be all the more full, but you cannot fail at this game of life.

Life simply is, so have fun, why don't you? Relax and ask to see things differently today.

*March 25*

## FLYING HIGH

Tis true what they say:
You cannot see the forest for the trees.
If only you could fly above
And see what the eagle sees!

Why then, my child, your view would change.
No longer would you fear.
For up so high when flying
All your answers would be clear.

The questions that you ponder now
Have all been answered, yet
You do not see this clearly
When your connection you forget.

Remembering is half the fun.
Ask the bird who flies
How free it feels to rise and soar
With abandon through the skies.

Leave your worries on the ground.
Rise above the body and you'll see
That never do you walk alone
When you fly with me.

This freedom is your birthright.
You've merely lost your way.
But take my hand, come fly with me
On this, Remembrance Day.

## ALL YOU EVER HAVE

Savor every moment of this existence, for now is all you have.

The past is over. Why do you carry it to this present moment? Doing so is a learned habit because you think all moments are connected and sequential. They are not. You create each moment anew. You need not connect each dot.

You are not happy now? Choose happiness ... now. "But I cannot be happy because such-and-such happened!" And there you err. There is only now. Isolate this moment and choose how to see it. Choose how to live it. Savor this moment. Savor this existence, for now is all you ever have. It is always your choice. That is how being a creator works.

*March 27*

## PEEKING THROUGH

In darkness you live, stumbling about, groping for truth, groping to find your way. You turn a corner and see a bit of light. It is refreshing, full of hope. It feels so very different.

You no longer can settle for darkness, and so you stumble on, but not quite so blindly any longer, until a bit more light reveals itself. Now you are beginning to change. You most definitely cannot go back to stumbling.

Truth is Light. The light is Love. Darkness, merely lack of understanding Truth … neither good nor bad, but oh so far from Light that you must move ever-onward toward full brightness, full knowing.

Seek the Light and you shall find it. Make the choice always for Light and you will be guided by that self-same Light, for it is the light of the Soul calling, and you are That. You have found the key. You have found your way Home.

## BARBS

Yes, wire can be used to keep creatures in or out of a space, but at times it is believed that a simple fence is not enough. Then the barbs are added. Humans know that inflicting pain will keep others out.

Barbs inflict pain. Do you not at times do the same with your words? Your actions and body language alone at times are enough to fence yourself off and keep others away. Then you add the barbs. Oh yes, they most certainly can inflict pain and are most effective at keeping others away.

What would happen if you took down the fence? Why, then you would be vulnerable. Or, so you think. The truth is, then you would be free, my friend. Think of your Great Plains before there were fences. Such freedom! Fences and barbs cause separation and division where there truly is none.

You have no need for fences in your life. You are fully safe and loved without them. And with no fences—with no false separation—there can be no place for barbs. Where there is openness, there is freedom. Where there is freedom, love reigns.

*March 29*

GUIDED

Allow yourself to be guided. We ask you to picture a blind man. The blind man has a choice. He can use a cane and swing it blindly in front of him, feeling about for dangers and obstacles. He can also choose to use the senses of another in the form of a guiding dog.

With total trust in the consciousness of another, the blind man now steps forward, led by love ... the unconditional love of his guide. He no longer stumbles about, knowing the dog will not let him stumble. There is a bond between them based on trust, based on love, based on service.

Can you put your hand on the lead of the One who is there to guide you? Can you step out with full trust that you will not stumble? It takes training to work with Your Guide. The cues are subtle, but always are they present, for Your Helper never leaves your side.

Reach out. Trust. Step forward as a team—a true partnership, bonded by love—and be guided.

## REACHING HIGHER THAN TOLERANCE

You speak of religious tolerance. We ask you to feel this word, "tolerance." Does it not have a bit of a negative vibration? Do you not "tolerate" bad behavior or a naughty child? Do you not "tolerate" medicine? We ask you to see others' spiritual beliefs and all beliefs which differ from your own in a more positive light. Are not beliefs merely different modes of perception? What is wrong and right varies from one mind to another. Is not all that exists merely an expression of the One Mind?

Do not merely tolerate others' beliefs, but look for what they can teach you. All religions at a basic level share certain Truths, for these Truths come from inner teachings. Those which may come from human distortions can be discarded by your individual mind through the act of loving discernment, meaning that you give it the heart test.

How does it feel?

If you choose to discard a certain belief, do so not with mere tolerance, but with "compassionate allowing," as you see beyond the belief to the Spirit-essence of all beings. Then you do not merely tolerate all others. Then you allow yourself to love thy brother as thyself, and to thereby love God with all your heart.

*March 31*

## NEW SIGHT

As one ages, the physical body changes. There can be growth in this. All experience exists to produce growth. We wish you to take the changing eyes as an example. As a child, the eyes are sharp and see all physical objects with great clarity. As an experienced adult, one no longer sees physical objects with great clarity.

You may stare at a plate of food and perceive it in one way until you place before the eyes a set of spectacles. Lo! Behold! The plate before you now appears to hold objects which before were completely imperceptible. Did the plate change or did you? Or did nothing change save your perception?

Perception truly is reality, no matter in which dimension you find yourself. We wish you simply to realize that reality is subjective. There are billions of realities … infinite realities … all yours for the making, yours for the taking, and all existing to produce growth.

The aging process does not bring about death, but growth! Through the experience of the changing eyesight you have achieved spiritual understanding and now see with greater clarity of a different sort. Is that not growth? You are still here. You will always be "here," for you exist eternally. Only your "here" changes as your perception changes.

## CHOOSING

Why does it feel good to judge others? Because it satisfies the ego's goals. Ego cannot survive if you see all others as spirit beings. Ego must make you see yourself as a separate, superior being if it is to survive. It continuously whispers in your ear, nudging you to look around you and see the differences. It even makes you feel good for doing so.

Do not feel guilty. You are certainly not alone in feeling separate. There are billions of egos running about, desperately protecting themselves. And when they see a light that shines, they run for cover. Gossip is a key weapon of ego; judgment another.

Awareness is a key defense of the spirit, which sits quietly, waiting to be remembered and recognized. When awareness tugs at your mind, showing you that ego is at it again, then you can make a choice. Which aspect of you do you wish to honor today: truth or deception? The choice is always up to you.

*April 2*

## NO PARADOX

Duality ... a state of here and there at once. You are both of everything (hot and cold, good and bad, happy and sad), yet you can only focus on and experience one thing at a time in your present condition, and so you believe there is a paradox. There is no paradox. You are all that is all at once.

The paradox is an illusion of living in a state in which consciousness is not fully expanded. This intense focus causes you to fix yourself here or there, but not both and everything in between at the same time. It is merely a matter of perspective ... of focus.

Enjoy the here while you are here. Go "there" when you wish with your consciousness and leave "here" here. When you have gone "there" enough times in your consciousness whilst still here, moving twixt the two, then your consciousness will become so flexible that you can simply be here, there, and everywhere here and now.

Then you will know there is no paradox at all as duality dissolves.

## ROOTED

Why do you dig in your heels? Because you are quite earthbound when you do so. It is the human side of you that has such set ideas that you take your very human heels and dig them quite firmly into the very earthly ground and stand that ground. And what does this gain you? A sense of separation and righteousness.

What happens when you look down upon your humanness from the viewpoint of yourself as spirit? Why, you become so light that you rise up and float right out of those firmly planted feet. From there you not only can relieve the tension of being so firmly rooted in your position, but you may even smile to see all the others rooted in place. And then you may even laugh to see how interconnected you all are at the roots beneath all the surface differences. But of course you cannot see this until you rise above.

*April 4*

## YOUR CHOICE

"Do as we say, not as you do" -- a bit of a twist on one of your sayings. So often you march off through your day acting on your own, as if you are connected to naught but your own mind. Then, when you err or encounter difficulties, you wonder why.

We are there whispering in your ear at all times, yet you turn down the volume and rush off to do it your own way. This is fine. This is how you learn, but how long would you like to run around in circles?

Life is cyclical, this is true, but would you like it to be for you as an ever-expanding spiral or as a small closed circle like that upon which your hamsters run, getting nowhere? You pray for guidance, then fail to listen to or for our answers.

That which you call intuition is our greatest voice. Start there, for from that point the guidance oft gets more subtle, but the more you trust, the louder the voices. Listen well.

## PERCEPTION

What is a hallucination? It is when one perceives something with the physical eyes that others say is not real. What is real? What the mass consciousness has agreed upon. And so, when one person has an apparition that others have not, then the one is suffering from delusion. You all fear standing out from a crowd, and so you accept blithely the accepted reality.

What if Jesus or Mary were to appear before you? Would this be a hallucination or a gift? Again we ask: What is real? The reality you accept is nothing but a projection of consciousness that the brain perceives a certain way … a hologram of sorts. There are many realities.

Do away with the brain and you will experience a whole new version of reality. It will not be a hallucination. In fact, some would call it Heaven.

*April 6*

## WOW

"Wow" – a word you say when you experience amazement. There is no judgment in "wow," no good or bad implied, simply wow. Wow is healthy. It shows that you are merely observing events around you. The interpretation is one of surprise, but not condemnation or jubilation.

When all around you seems to be "going to hell," as you say, step back, blink a few times, and instead of screaming and crying, say, "Wow." This buys you time to breathe. Now you can say, "Isn't that interesting!" and see things more clearly from the greater perspective.

Equally, when events exceed your greatest expectations or previous experience, you can respond the same. "Wow" keeps you in the middle of extreme ends of duality. In the middle there is peace. From the middle it is far easier to respond with love.

May your entire life be one great wow.

## IMPATIENCE

You wait and wait, and that for which you wait does not happen. Your frustration rises. Do you not yet understand that if it has not yet happened there is a reason? Frustration is a human emotion. It stems from impatience.

Impatience ... "lack of patience" may as well be called lack of trust. All is in perfect order. Frustration is a sign that you have not yet learned or you have forgotten this.

You have your eyes set on a specific goal or a particular timing of that goal. If it is not unfolding according to your vision, then trust that your vision is not in the best interest of the Whole. When you have gained that level of trust, impatience and frustration go away.

Trust us. You will look back on this and say, "Now I see." And you will see that your frustration was a wasted opportunity to trust and be at peace.

*April 8*

## ALL ABOUT PERSPECTIVE

As you prepare for one you love to pass to the next chapter of life you struggle. It is not easy for you to let go. They are off on a new journey. For them it is a fresh start, to be filled with wonder. For you, you are left with a new start as well, filled with absence, if that is how you choose to see it.

See with new eyes. See through their eyes and rejoice in this passage. Walk at their side in your mind's eye and marvel at the wonders. They are still alive … perhaps not in the sense that you know here, but more fully alive than ever before. Feel the love that surrounds them. Is this not what you have always wanted for your loved ones? Rejoice. You grieve only for yourself. Do you see this?

Shift your consciousness to that of your loved one, and there can be no grief. Envy, perhaps, but your time will come. For now, a small shift in perspective will make your journey less challenging. It is all about perspective.

We love you so very much. There is no need to suffer.

## OPPORTUNITIES

There will always be challenges in your life. How you handle them is what matters.

See them not as challenges, but opportunities. If, when faced with a challenge, you shrink back, run away if you can, cry, and complain, then you have missed the point. Even if you did not call this upon yourself at a conscious level, it has presented itself.

How can you grow from it? Merely by seeing it as an opportunity.

Life is so much easier with the tiniest change in perspective.

*April 10*

## FROM THIS MOMENT ON

"From this moment on" … may this be your mantra for today.

Do not drag yourself through the mud for past transgressions or regrettable decisions. Apply what you know now to be Truth and do your best. "But I was doing my best then!" you cry, and we ask you, were you? If so, then it should be even easier to forgive yourself. If not, then from this moment on remember what you know in your heart and apply it with diligence.

Most importantly, love yourself. See yourself with compassion, just as you would see any child who makes mistakes. Now pick yourself up, dust yourself off, and smile. Do not take yourself so seriously.

There. Isn't that better?

## ALARMING

Everything vibrates, including you. If something vibrates at exactly the rate as you do, you will not notice it. Think of your cellular phone—its very vibration is used as an alarm. It vibrates to get your attention. You vibrate to get others' attention, do you not? Your body vibrates to get your attention. It is hard to concentrate with all of this vibrating going on, but you cannot get away from it, for all is vibration.

How do you wish to be felt: as a loud, annoying, dissonant vibration or as a soft caress that is soothing and welcomed? You control your own vibration. In fact, the evolution of your personal frequency is the reason you are here. If that very thought is alarming, then you know exactly where to start.

*April 12*

## THE POWER OF PRAYER

What happens when you pray? You set in motion a vibration. Thoughts are aspects of consciousness, and consciousness is the creative force of the universe—that aspect of mind which you share with the One Divine Mind. Using your consciousness in prayer, you create a link between you and that which you desire.

Imagine a circuit between you and the desired outcome as a thing. Until the prayer, this circuit exists in potentiality, but is unlighted. Through the act of prayer, you activate this circuit and it lights up. Seen now by your helpers, acknowledged by the Divine Mind, all forces can now conspire to activate whatever other circuitry is needed to fulfill this desire, this prayer.

Of course it is not exactly like this, but quite similar, and you do enjoy your analogies. We wish you to understand how very powerful are your thoughts and prayers. Light up the sky with prayers of peace and love for all mankind. This type of prayer—that which benefits the greater good—carries the greatest power. Never forget that you carry this Power within you.

## THE PERFECT INSTRUMENT

The one known as St. Francis of Assisi did pray to be an instrument of the Lord. What does this mean? An instrument is a tool—an implement used to affect and change something for a desired result.

If God were to use you, what result would God desire? You know the answer, as did St. Francis: to bring more peace and love to your world. How can you be such an instrument? It is quite simple. Allow God's love to flow in you and through you. Do not dam it up with thoughts that are less than loving and peaceful. Judge not others. Merely be that perfect instrument through which love flows unimpeded, reaching out to others so that they may experience love in its most pure form.

You do not need to be a saint to do this, for all spirit-beings have this capacity. Be the instrument of God which you are in every moment and let the love flow.

## THE VOICE INSIDE

You hear a tiny voice inside.
From this voice you cannot hide.
Is it your imagination?
Then why such utter fascination?

Have you not asked, "Are You there?
Do You truly know my every hair?
Is it You who whispers in my ear?
The One so many were taught to fear?"

"How can this be the voice of God?
Why do I find this thought so odd?"
It is the result of your false teaching.
For a human God you have been reaching.

Your God is not in human form.
To no set image does God conform.
You can't conceive of what God is
When using words like "He" and "His."

Release the need to understand
That which lies beyond the hand.
Simply know this Force is real.
It's something you can only feel.

For this, surrender is a must
If you will truly learn to trust.
The messages you thought you heard
When God did give to you a Word.

## THE ROAD YOU'RE ON

All of life is filled with strife. Welcome it. How boring would be an existence where nothing ever changed. Are you not supremely proud of yourself when you overcome adversity? Yes, but you would rather not have had that experience, you say. We understand. It is natural to want to run away from pain. But pain reminds you how enjoyable is pleasure. Activity reminds you how dull is inactivity.

Pain is a necessary part of growth, but it is a sliding scale. Just how painful is that pain depends on the focus you give it and the thoughts with which you surround it. Experience the bumps. Acknowledge them, and then drive through them to smoother roads instead of stalling or slowing down. "Ah, that way was quite the experience. May I never pass that way again. But if I do, I have learned the best way around."

Grow from the pain. This is the point. And whilst on the smooth path, appreciate that experience with gratitude. It's a wonderful life—bumps and all.

## THROUGH THICK AND THIN

Sitting in the darkness
You doubt that we are here.
But it is your intention
That always draws us near.

All of life is like this,
A play of your emotion.
Your wish is our desire.
We thrive on your devotion.

We only wish to serve you.
At times it's like a test.
For when you also wish to serve
The results are always best.

So, you see, it's quite a team
That we and you do make.
Working thus in harmony,
A simple give and take.

We give love, you take it.
We appreciate yours, too.
For, helping you to learn to love
Is why we come to you.

So count on us to be there
Through all things thick and thin.
At your side your angels fly,
If you will only let us in.

## GUIDANCE

A single step propels you in new directions. You can make the choice to step out at any time, but it does take courage.

You know not what the future holds, but you do know what your heart tells you. Listen there first. Its voice is far more accurate than the mind, which is ruled by ego. The heart is not ruled, but fueled by love. It has a mind of its own, and never will it steer you wrong.

Listen to your heart first and foremost before you step out blindly. The heart will guide you always as you place one foot in front of the other. It will light the way, and your path will shine ever brighter.

*April 18*

## ON RIGHT AND WRONG

You have an expression, "Do not waste your breath." To you this means to try fruitlessly to defend yourself. This is good advice. What purpose does it do to state your case? Does it matter if one is right and another wrong? What if both are right in their own minds?

What does "right" mean? You give it meaning and then become stuck in defending that meaning. And what if the meaning should change, as surely it will, for all things change as growth is experienced.

And so, the effort spent in defending one's actions, thoughts, and words served what purpose? To antagonize another? To make another feel better or worse? Is it your goal to show another how to think? Why do you feel the need to do so?

Surrender and allow all to think as they will, including yourself. You cannot waste a breath, for with each breath you experience and learn. Once again we advise you to step back and see with compassion for all others as well as yourself, for you are learning through the angst and through the joy.

All is in perfect order. Relax and live with joy.

## CO-DIRECTORS

There is so much sorrow in your world. Know that it is not of God. God is all goodness, all love. "Does such a thing exist?" you ask when you are surrounded by evidence of the opposite.

You are placing too much faith in an illusion. You are believing the dream is real. "But it is real!" you insist. "I can touch it and see it!" Yes, but is your body even real? Is the picture on the television screen the real scene? It creates emotions as if it were real, but it is not real. It is a projection. Your life as a human is a projection on a screen. You change the play with your consciousness, but not at the level of the human. The actors on the screen do not change the script. This is done at a higher level, with the approval of the director. The greater the skill of the actor, the more leeway and interaction given to him by the Director.

Learn to increase your interaction with the Director of this life—this projection onto the screen you call planet Earth. Do you not know of your movies where star and director are one and the same? They have reached a level of competence of moving about the stage, and so can you. Work toward this goal and the play itself becomes all the more enjoyable.

## YOUR VITAL ROLE

Lights come on. The stage is lit.
Where in this drama do you fit?
Are you to be a small, bit actor,
Or in your life a major factor?

Do not discount your vital role.
So important is your soul.
For each such love he has to share,
And in this way your soul lay bare.

Yes, on a stage you do this act
Where all can see how you react
To life's ordeals—the ups and downs
In which you play both victims and clowns.

When all the acting gets too hard,
Step off the stage and just regard
The drama and action and stage design
While you consider your next vital line.

Don't get wrapped up in all the drama,
The murder and mayhem and also the trauma.
Watch with compassion as life goes by
On the stage where nothing can ever really die.

## ENOUGH

"Am I loving enough?" This most simple of phrases can get you through the most difficult of times. If the answer to this question is yes, then you are placing your focus on what is most important. You are allowing love to flow. If the answer is no, then you are now aware that somewhere within you is a blockage of that most powerful of elixirs.

What is "enough"? When it comes to love, there is no limit. "Loving fully" comes close to the answer. If you ask yourself, "Am I loving enough?" whenever you remember to do so, and you are loving fully, then you will find peace. When you love with all your heart and soul, you have loosed your True Self and found authenticity.

Are you loving enough? Start with yourself—a good place to begin—and move on from there. Peace awaits on this most joyous of journeys.

*April 22*

## THE FIRST AND ONLY CAUSE

All things have a cause, for all that you experience is an effect. Cause and effect, the two constants.

What is the First Cause of all that is? It is Love. Love is the intent behind the first thought, the first word, the first action. All else has flowed from that Love-Cause. If, somewhere along the way in your experience of Love in Expression, you have not experienced love or are currently experiencing less than love, go back to the very beginning of time, before your world existed. Go back and ask to experience what it felt like to birth a universe. You would be overcome by the vibration, by the explosion of such energy.

Those around you and those who came before you were given free will. This may have been abused. But all is going according to plan, for in forgetting the First Cause and getting lost, you must find your way back home. Anything less than being the Presence of Love, your First Cause, is illusion. Do not get lost in the illusion.

Travel back in time and merge your mind with the Mind that had love as its intention. In this remembrance of your true Home and your true Cause, you will awaken love within yourself. Now express that love and see what effects you cause.

## NEW BEGINNINGS

New beginnings. Each moment of your life is one. You may as well celebrate this moment, for it represents a fresh start. If you find yourself grieving, you are focusing on the past. "No. This moment now is unbearable!" you cry, and that is because your perceptions are based upon a belief system focused around past experiences.

What if you had been dropped into an alien world and new nothing of this culture? You could only rely upon what you know. So, what do you know? "I AM. I exist. I feel drawn to connect. What is this magnetic pull that causes me to want to communicate and interact?" It is your true nature calling. Love is the connective tissue between all of you. It is the savior within you when you feel that all is lost and you are lost.

Save yourself in times of trouble and save yourself a lot of trouble by dwelling not in the past. Peer not into the future, and see the present moment through new eyes: through the eyes of love.

*April 24*

## SACRED AND HOLY

Evil does exist in your world, but not in the form of a devil any more than God is in the form of a bearded man in the clouds. There is no horned being with a pitchfork, no dark, bearded man with a glint in his eye.

Evil is the result of a complete lack of understanding of who and what the human truly is. It is a lack of understanding that the human body cloaks the sacred, holy spirit. If one recognized the Spirit within others, one would bow down on their knees and worship That. If one truly recognized the Spirit within themselves, they would revere every breath they took as sacred. They would honor the body as sacred and care for it with utmost respect. Acts of evil would be impossible.

And so, what you know as evil is nothing more than ignorance and misunderstanding. Have compassion for those who commit evil, for they are blind and deaf to the spirit within themselves and others. It is not anger and judgment that will change them or their acts, but love and forgiveness. You may not see the effects of your love and forgiveness in one who is profoundly blind and deaf in this lifetime, but you will have honored the Spirit, and there is no greater act than this.

## UNTIL YOU MEET AGAIN

Grief is a process. This you know. It has certain stages. You cannot escape grief when you have lost one who is dear to you, and why would you want to? Yes, we know: because it feels so very awful. The pain at times seems unbearable.

Do you not see that grief is in proportion to how much you have loved? Your world is one of polarities. You are here to experience the full spectrum of feelings so as to fully know love. You touch grief and then you know it. Now you know how very much you loved.

The problem comes when you remain in a grief state. This is when understanding the truth that your loved ones still exist will help you to rise above the pain. They are still with you. You can feel them when you expand your beliefs and train the mind to be silent. Know also that you will see them again. Their love still surrounds you.

In the meantime, your famous bard was quite correct. Is it not better to have loved and temporarily lost, than not to have loved that one at all? The pain will lessen. Bring them into your heart and hold them there until you meet again.

*April 26*

## SPECIAL TOUCHES

Give and take ... you know this as a rule of life. When there is balance there is harmony.

Give, give, give of your love, not so that you will get more in return, but because you world is out of balance. Believe us, give more and the more you will receive. It is the Law of Balance. You want more love in your life? More companionship, more of anything? Then give. It cannot help but come back to you. Nothing that you want is outside of yourself. You have created all that you have with your consciousness, which is never separate from yourself.

What do you want? See yourself as having this now. Begin giving of that from the mind and most especially from the heart. Then you may prepare for the taking.

Give and take ... it is a matter of balance.

## BEYOND

You do not like strife? You do not like the feel of conflict? Some do. If you do not, it is due to your level of sensitivity to the vibrations around you. All is energy.

Some flinch in the face of dissonant vibrations, which is all that strife is. Some are energized by them. Some run away. Some lash back. If none of these are desired reactions to dissonance, go <u>beyond</u> the vibrations. We ask you to note the particular use of the word "beyond," for some of you would not like the word "above," fearing a feeling of superiority.

In the face of dissonant vibrations, recognize that your consciousness is firmly focused at the human level, where thoughts are felt as dense energy that vibrates in relation to each other. In this awareness, shift your consciousness beyond the human level to the finer level of pure spirit. There, beyond the fray is a place of non-duality. There can be no relativity there beyond ... no judgment ... simply "being."

In the face of dissonance, you can always shift beyond to the state of peace and pure love and simply "be."

*April 28*

## PRECIOUS METAL

Hold your head high through all of your challenges. What is it that makes you want to run and hide when the road gets bumpy? You have a reputation, you say? Based upon what? On what others think? On what labels and ideas you have built up around yourself in your mind?

Did you come into this life with a reputation? In a way, you did ... a reputation of pure love. But that has become degraded by the human ideas of right and wrong. Hold your head high as you face challenges. This is why you are here—to be forged by fire as the strong rod of gold that you are. Bend not under the heat, but stand tall and remember, you are precious metal, indeed.

Now find the mettle to face others who may not see how you glitter inside. Hold your head high and shine no matter what. You cannot fail the test. Life is about growing in love. There is no shortage of opportunities to do so.

Begin by loving yourself.

## OUTCOMES

Get yourself out of the way when you are having difficulties accomplishing a task. It is the ego which causes blockages. Always remind yourself, "I by myself do nothing. I as a part of the Greater Self have limitless power."

Take less credit for your accomplishments and give credit where it is due—to the Higher Intelligence which flows through you at all times. It is God, Spirit, the Divine Mind which animates you. That is where your power comes from. Surrender to this power and see your personal power increase.

Let not your heart be troubled when things do not go your way. Surrender and ask to be guided. Then, sit back and relax without worry. Take action as you are guided, but now it is without effort. There is never a need to struggle. Struggle is merely a sign that you are allowing ego over Spirit to be in control. You already know the outcome when this is so.

You may not always know the outcome when you allow God to run the show, but you can trust that it will be Divine.

*April 30*

## A REASON TO REJOICE

There is no substitute for experience. You may think you understand another's grief, but until you experience the death of one you hold dear, you cannot fully understand how another suffers. You may think you know what pain is, but until you suffer yourself, you do not fully understand.

As a spirit, all is love and light. As an earthly being (for just a while a role you play, mind you), you have the opportunity to experience pain as well as full health; grief as well as celebration and joy. Yes, your life has its share of ups and downs. That is why you are here—for the experience.

Do not wallow in the grief and pain. Experience it. Learn from it. Acknowledge it, and then rise above. Once you have pulled yourself up, now you can do the same for others. All others are here for the same reason: to experience duality and grow from it.

Rejoice! You are alive!

*May 1*

## UNFOLDING BEAUTIFULLY

There is no harm in waiting. All does not have to be done at once. How does a flower open, but by unfolding? You are in the process of unfolding. Do not rush the process, but do it in a patient, orderly fashion, watching the perfection.

Allow nature to take its course. You cannot rush a seed to sprout. Why would you rush your development? Could it be because you have experienced a taste of the bliss that comes with knowing who you are? So now you are dissatisfied. Is that it? This is a good thing. That blissful feeling is not finite. It is not going anywhere. That, my friend, is love vibrating more fully than you normally experience in your seedling state.

Nurture your growth, knowing that growth is occurring as you love. Enjoy the journey and relax. All is in perfect order.

# May 2

## IN ALIGNMENT

Why does it feel good to do good things?

It is not a reward. It is because you are in alignment with your Source, with your True Self. There is order in alignment. There is resonance. The Universe sings when there is resonance.

Nothing is ever so important that you cannot stop what you are doing to help another. In helping another you align with your Source, for in truth, there is no other. It is merely the right hand helping the left hand of the same Body.

Resonance. Alignment. Harmony. All part of the experience of this song of Life.

## ALONG THE SPECTRUM

All of life exists along a spectrum of vibration of Consciousness. The higher the vibration, the closer you come to the experience of bliss—of perfection—of the totality of God. Just as in the physical world you can only perceive a limited segment of the spectrum of electromagnetic energy, light, and colors, so it is that because of the density of the physical body you can only perceive a limited segment of the whole of Consciousness here, even though Consciousness makes up your very soul.

The greatest bliss you can experience now is but a tiny speck of the glory that awaits you. That is why you call it Heaven and innately know there is something so much better. Heaven is not a place, but a state of consciousness. You create your own heaven on earth from moment to moment by your choice of thoughts, beliefs, and actions. You slide up and down the scale of consciousness from moment to moment using your will. What WILL you experience today? Will it be heaven or hell? It is always a choice.

Know that you enter into the so-called Heaven vibrating as a soul at the very state of consciousness or level of vibration that your soul earned here. So, unless you are quite content with your use of will and love at this point, do not be in a hurry. Work on perfecting your thoughts now so that you will enter the next phase at an even higher point on the spectrum. Yes, you will be surrounded by love no matter at what level you enter, but the greater your love here and now, the more heavenly the experience ever after. It is all one spectrum leading to the same place: Home.

# May 4

## FROM THE START

Can you imagine if all young children were informed that they were living expressions of God ... that they need not look up to a figure in the sky and earn His favor, but instead be the living embodiment of the loving Force here on earth?

And what if all children were taught that the other children they encounter were made up of that self-same essence? What kind of world would that engender? Then they might just pick up a toy gun and ask, "What is this for?" It would make no sense to them.

You have your work cut out for you, do you not? Do not become discouraged. Be the presence of Love in every moment, and start a revolution.

## GROWTH

You go through childhood with such innocence. The body grows along the way and changes. It does this by itself. You need make no effort and you grow taller and fill out. The body continues to renew itself moment by moment, cell by cell.

Why would the spirit not also continuously grow? That is life: constant growth. You as spirit are also constantly changing. That is why you exist. The body goes from small to large. The spirit increases in vibration. The higher vibration reflects a more loving soul, for love is the highest of all vibrations.

You stunt your physical growth by poisoning the body with toxic substances and lack of exercise. You stunt the spirit body by absorbing and giving off the lower vibrations of judgment, hate, and anger.

How tall do you wish to grow? Ingest a daily diet of loving kindness. Shower it freely upon others and bring full health to the human-spirit body. It is a team effort.

*May 6*

## BIRD'S EYE VIEW

Why is trust such a hard thing for you to learn? Because in the past you have trusted and have suffered a perceived hurt or things did not go as you planned. "You" is the important term in this case. There is a little "you" and a "You" that is far grander. Whilst focused on the human side, when things do not go as you intended, you see this as failure. What does the greater You see? The greater Self sees the big picture.

Whilst standing in the puzzle, you only see the adjacent pieces. Step above the card table, and now you see the entire picture as it comes together. "Aha!" you say. "Now I see! I wanted to place a certain shaped piece next to me, but it fits far better over there. The best piece for this situation is lying yonder."

Do you get it now? That which you considered failure is only so when seen with limited vision. Trust that all is in perfect order always, and a door that closes or fails to open is doing exactly what it should for the greater good.

Relax and trust. Surrender and allow. Oh, such peace that comes when you rise above the smaller self!

## HALFWAY

"I'll meet you halfway." We speak now not of compromise, in which two humans give in a bit of their wants to help each other out, but a meeting of spirit and ego. Picture our world of spirit and your world of matter. You think that they are separate, but they intermingle completely, for all is energy.

You think that you cannot connect with the realm of spirit, but you are in it all the time. It is most accessible to you in your dreams. And so we advise you to compromise. We will meet you halfway ... somewhere between full waking and fully asleep. You can experience this state at will. You call it meditation. It is merely a time to shift your consciousness from the material and go within the silence.

There you can connect with All That Is and experience true love for yourself. So you see, in this instance, meeting halfway is not a compromise at all, but experiencing the fullness of life itself.

*May 8*

PENNIES FROM HEAVEN


Pick a penny off the street
A piece of copper that you've found.
Coincidence or just plain luck
To find it on the ground?

You look for signs in all you see
Signs to show you're not alone.
A penny or a butterfly
That comes to you from points unknown.

The signs are all around you,
Yet often you don't see
The messages we send you
You call it "synchronicity."

But it's not luck or chance, you see,
That brings these gifts to you
But love that's sent from Spirit.
It's our way of getting through.

So scoff not at those who see the signs.
They're simply more aware,
And notice how we speak to them,
Producing pennies from thin air.

It's easy to manipulate
The things you see with your plain eyes.
So open them and see our gifts
When we send you a surprise.

YOUR ESSENCE

Your Source is not separate from you, but It is larger than you. Feel It settle in your heart, this presence, this Christ Consciousness, this knowing that God is not a being, that God is "being," itself.

Can you worship that? You need not worship at all. Simply participate in that joyous unfolding of existence—of Life in all its glory. You are that. The real you is Life, itself. We are not talking of a body. We are not talking of a mind. Never mind the name or labels. These are what hold you back from knowing your magnificence. Let them all go, and what remains? Existence. Love. Being. That is God. But that being-ness is not separate. It is your essence.

Do you see now? Go forth this day with joy in knowing this. Do not shout to the world with exuberance in your joy, "I am God!" for many will not understand. And until you can look upon the poorest beggar and the mightiest tyrant and say, "And that is God as well," then you do not understand.

Until you can look beyond all external appearances and all physical actions and see the true essence of Being-ness in all things, then we simply ask you to express love in all you do. Do this and realization will come.

## *May 10*

### PEACE IS THE PRIZE

Suddenly a thought occurs to you. You have forgotten to do this or that, or you focus on how much work lies ahead. Suddenly you are no longer able to enjoy yourself. The body tenses. What has happened? You were in the now, but now your consciousness has shifted to a future event. You are taking care of the task in your mind at some time in the future, and you have lost your equanimity.

It is well and good to plan. Take time to do this. But when you are involved in an enjoyable task, keep your focus in the present. It is quite easy to lose your sense of peace. Merely shift your focus to the past or future.

If you can learn to be entirely present, more peace will be the prize.

## GOALS

Healthy, wealthy, and wise. Laudable goals for a human being.

Is one more preferable than another? What would you gain from attaining each? If it is power, we ask you to examine your motives more closely. If it is peace, then you are on the right track. What good are health, wealth, and wisdom if they bring not peace? What good are they if not used to spread that peace and joy to others?

More and more and more wealth and wisdom will not bring about more and more and more peace. Money is a thing. Peace is a state. Wisdom helps you to attain this. The measure of true wisdom is how it is used to bring more goodness into your world. Health follows peace in most cases, but not all, for certain life lessons must be learned through illness. There is the matter of karmic debt, a very real thing. This is when peace becomes a goal even greater than health.

If you can be healthy or unhealthy, wealthy or poor, wise or not and still find peace, then you have a treasure beyond words. How to attain this oft-elusive peace? Sit in the silence, my friend, and ask that question of God. Repeat this practice until you have your answer.

*May 12*

## TRUE VS. FALSE

Do you not understand that the devil is a human creation and not a reality? God is. God is all that is. God is all goodness and love. THAT is the only power that is.

All else is a lack of God-power. "How can this be?" you ask. What is darkness? Is it a real thing? Does it have power? No. It is merely the lack of light. What is evil? Is it a real power? No. It is merely a lack of Love.

The devil exists only within human consciousness, and only if you allow this false creation into your reality. To the one who truly knows God, the devil is not a power.

Evil is a human trait. Rise above your humanness to the conscious vibration of Spirit. There you will find no evil and no devil, for imbued with the consciousness of Light, there can be no darkness.

*May 13*

UNIQUE

Do not concern yourself so much with the spiritual growth of others. Have you not enough to learn yourself? Others will come along at their own pace, like a seed sprouting. You cannot rush it. Most importantly, why do you want to? Is it because you want to feel more peace when in their presence? Then is this your challenge or theirs?

It is the responsibility of no other to bring you peace. Is it because you want others to experience the happiness and peace you have found? A laudable goal, but could any other have told you in words how to get to the place where you find yourself now? Perhaps a grain of wisdom here or there would have helped you, but it was your path … earned step by precious step. Would you have had another push you down it?

Relax and enjoy your own journey. Enjoy observing others on their own. Should they ask for your help, take them by the hand and give them a gentle nudge, then let go. It is all about the journey.

Although all spirit is One, in this experience you call the human life each being is here to experience it in their own way. That is how you grow—like a wall of individually shaped stones, with each contributing their own unique shape to the whole.

*May 14*

LISTEN

Purity of thought
and clarity of mind
Lead to ideas that run through your head
That are of the loving kind.

From whence come these thoughts
That you do not control?
The answer is quite simple:
From the center of your soul.

You so often fail to listen
When quiet thoughts they do appear.
For unlike your mental chatter
These subtle thoughts are not so clear.

The Voice it seems like part of you
And for this reason you don't heed
The words it whispers in your ear—
The ones you truly need.

The still, small voice is part of you
Not separate or aloof.
And as you learn to follow it
It will send you, oh, such proof.

"Abide in me!" it calls to you.
"Of you I am a part.
To trust my voice is simple
Merely tune in to your heart."

## NO COINCIDENCE

That is how it works: You reach out and grab the hand of a stranger in a moment of desperation. "Hear my story. I don't know what to do!" And that one to whom you reached out has just the answer you need, even though she has no idea why your paths crossed at that instant.

Once again, it is all clear from the greater picture. Step above the scene where one seeming individual reaches out to another, and you will see a network much like the cells in your body, all interacting, all helping the whole. You are so intimately interconnected, yet you do not see this at your level.

It is almost comical, your reactions to what you call "coincidence." Instead of reacting with surprise, there will come a time when you react to synchronicity with a nod of the head and say, "There we go again—intersecting—we cells in the body of God. Isn't it beautiful?"

Go on bumping into each other and enjoy your little "coincidences." It is all part of the fun, the joy, and the discovery that all is One.

## May 16

### THAT ONE . . . YOUR NEW FRIEND

Do you love yourself enough? Do you? Do you speak to yourself lovingly and regard yourself with compassion? Take a step back and see yourself from afar. Listen to the way that one you call "me" is addressing itself.

Do you want to step in and say, "Please be more kind"? Is that one being patient and understanding with themself? Do you want to step in and say, "There, there. You are far more worthy than you are giving yourself credit for"? Do you see now how easy it is to befriend and love that one who you have forsaken?

There are things you would never say to your lover, your friend, your beloved child, for they would be too hurtful, yet you say these things to that one -- God's beloved child – all the time. Step outside of the ego, who can be quite the unloving critic. You do not need that kind of friend. Now, from this new vantage point, befriend yourself.

Take yourself by the hand and say, "I am sorry I have forsaken you. I want to get to know you anew and truly take care of you. I love you just as our Father loves you. Please forgive me." And it is done.

Do you see how simple it is to turn your life around?
.

## CHOICE

Be very clear about what it is you desire, for your thoughts will bring you what you envision. Look around you. Everything you have and see is there by choice, either yours or another's.

If you are unhappy with what you see, then you must make a choice, mustn't you? Making choices takes courage. Not making the difficult choice is also a choice, is it not? You have chosen this life as you. There are lessons to be learned as you. Are you unhappy with you? Make a choice to change. You cannot change others around you? Then make a choice to change your thoughts about them.

You are not as powerless as you imagined. Choose to be happy. Choose to be loving. The two go hand-in-hand. Choose love as your companion to every thought, deed, and word, and you will walk hand-in-hand with the One who gave you this life in the first place.

## May 18

### CAN YOU HEAR ME NOW?

Why do you not speak enough of love? You speak of war, and crime, and atrocities, for all of these resonate to the lower vibrational field. Love is the highest vibration. It exerts a pull that you would know as magnetic upon all of you. It is why you are drawn to some and repelled by others, for all do not vibrate at the same frequency.

Most do not talk enough of love for fear of being ridiculed. "I love you" are the three most important words you can say. A mother discovers true love when she has a child and says these words freely to that child. This is because she shared the most intimate vibrational connection of the child in the womb.

You share this connection with the Higher Self which created you and which continues to give you life. "I love you," says this Source, yet you block this. You are loved beyond words, or you would not be here.

"I love you."
"I love you!"
"I LOVE YOU!"
"Can you hear Me now?"

Feel it now. Allow it to permeate every cell of your being, for it is You. You are Love and you are loved. If all listened carefully enough to hear it and feel it, there would be no wars; there would be no crimes. "I love you."

Roll in these words today. Repeat them to another, and then another, and then another. Maybe you will start something. Watch out. It might be catching. And then what would you do?

## FREE AND CLEAR

"Wash away my sins." Have you not heard this before? And some of you have been told to say it. This phrase has the ability to make you feel less worthy than you are. A better way of saying this would be, "Wash away my mistakes."

Picture yourself sitting in a shaft of white light. That Light which washes through you from above is the Life Force. It is called such because it animates you—it gives you Life. That Force is pure love. Were you not bathed in that Love, that Life Force, at all times, you would not breathe now in human form. Soak up that Love as it flows through you. It flows through you always, but when you sit in awareness and acknowledgement of its Presence and Strength, you call forth its healing powers.

Now repeat: "Wash away my mistakes," and it is done, for the greatest mistake you have made is believing that you are separate from this Force, from this Love. All other mistakes have followed from this Original Mistake. Let the Love flow through you now and cleanse you of anything less than love, forgiveness, and self-acceptance. See and feel the mistakes flowing down and out through this shaft until you are purified. Make this a daily or even hourly ritual, as needed, until you are free and clear—your pure and natural state.

*May 20*

## WORK TO DO

Arise! Arise from your self-imposed mediocrity!

You are not insignificant. If this seems like a new theme, you are correct, and we will repeat it until you understand your greatness. Does this mean you go about boasting? Not at all. That would be the opposite of what we are trying to show you.

Does it mean you stand tall within yourself and take stock of all of the negative things you have ever told yourself? Yes, please do so. Then gather all of these stones and stand at the top of a mountain in your mind. Roll them down, these stones you no longer need. Create an avalanche where no one will be harmed, but you will finally be free of these false beliefs you have accepted.

Arise now. You have work to do.

## BY THE HEART

Are you going to let others dictate how you feel?

"All is well. You have nothing to fear" ... words you would do well to live by. You have programmed your mind and hence your emotions to react to certain cues, and like a machine you do so. Step outside the role of an automated robot and live by the heart. How does it feel?

Only the heart is genuine from one moment to the next.

## May 22

### WIN - WIN

You lay to rest your most beloved. "How can I go on without them?" First, understand that they are not resting. They are more active than you are now that they no longer drag around that cumbersome body. They visit you often now, for when you think of them they feel it. It is you who feels sorrow, but do not feel it for the one who has moved on.

Treat yourself lovingly as you adjust to this new chapter in your life. The giant hole is mainly the physical presence. Fill this by bringing to mind all the more love you have experienced by having them in your life.

What will you do with that love? Why, go out and give it to those who need it—those who did not know the love you shared with your loved one. Translate what appears to be a loss into a gain on a greater scale. Give that love in memory of the one who still walks with you and you are allowing their love to live on.

You will see them again, and when you do, you can celebrate the loving use you put to the love they brought to this world. Now that is a win-win situation instead of a loss.

## BUZZING

Forgetfulness. Where do the thoughts go which you are trying to remember? They are still there. Thoughts are energy. They do not go away.

You must merely place the intention of matching the frequency of the concept you are trying to remember and send that intention outward. It will catch the intended thought as a fly to flypaper. You need simply let the intention do its job.

Do you wave flypaper around hoping to catch a random fly? What a sticky mess that would make! No. Once hung out there, you simply relax and allow it to work. When that which you are hoping to attract is caught you will know it.

Do you see how it works? The thoughts are no more in your brain than a fly is. They are buzzing around like the energy you hear crackling in high wires, for all is one great hive of energy.

*May 24*

## WITH PRACTICE

How does a musician improve? He practices scales over and over and over. Yes, the talent may be innate, but the practice perfects the skill.

As you awaken to who you are, you will want nothing more than to be the presence of love, but years of acting only as a human vs. a spirit-being will have habituated certain habits. How to overcome this? Practice, practice, practice.

You are aspiring to a new octave. This ascension does not come without a bit of effort on your part. Practice spreading love, being love, and seeing love unconditionally and soon you will be a virtuoso.

## POLARITY

How you view an event is completely up to you.

Does a tragedy—or what you interpret as a tragedy—propel you into action or lethargy, anger or compassion? Why are there so many choices? For yours is the realm of duality, of polar opposites.

The whole point of this existence is that you get to choose, and thus you either learn and grow or stagnate. There are other dimensions in which emotions have no role. This one which you now experience is one of the most difficult, the most arduous, due to its very dual nature.

We admire all of you for agreeing to take it on, for the learning you bring back with you from this experience is great. You have much to teach us all as a result of your experiences. Does this surprise you? Soldier on and pay attention to your choices. This is why you are here.

*May 26*

## ON US

Why are you so low? Why so down? Do you think you are alone? Does a flower grow by itself, or is it surrounded by all that it needs to flourish? Does a bear's hair thicken of its own accord in winter, or must the bear will it to do so?

You are never alone, my child. You do not have to think to breathe or blink, for you are so very well looked after. When things appear to go wrong, you do not have the greater vision, the bigger picture. As part of something far greater than yourself there is always interaction, give and take. What may appear to be a punishment is nothing of the sort.

Yes, question those things you cannot understand for now. All will be answered in time, from the realm of no-time, where some day you will look back with great understanding. You will see the vital role you played and that you never did play solitaire.

Take in a deep breath and know that the next one is on us.

## AS YOU MAKE IT

You want to know what heaven is like? You want to know what we do here? Spend some time in your dreams. It is a fanciful way of living and experiencing—full of wonder. You wonder a thing, and it becomes your experience, for all is consciousness without the impediment of a physical body or world.

You have experienced a bit of heaven in your so-called lucid dream state. You are almost focused in the physical world, but not quite, and so, you are aware that you are dreaming. In this semi-lucid state you control the dream experience, taking on form, environment, and role.

This is how you will experience consciousness when you no longer have a body. You wish to be with your loved ones, and you are. It is as real as your current reality. Never forget that reality is relative to the observer.

Be not afraid of death. It will be as beautiful as you make it.

*May 28*

INSPIRED

Any one of you could be inspired if you opened the spigot. Inspiration flows like water through you, but you control the flow. "Oh, I am not clever. Oh, I am not creative," you cry, and in so thinking you limit yourself.

You are all endowed with the characteristics of your Source, the Great Creator. Inspiration does not come from the human mind, but from the Spirit. Look at the origins of your word: In Spirit.

Be inspired today. Be in Spirit as you sit and connect with your Source. Do you wish to build something useful, write beautiful words, or draw something imaginative? Shift your focus from the limited mind of the human and assume the mantle of the limitless Mind.

## ANGELS AT YOUR SIDE

Angels are real, yes, indeed.
To help all of you when in need.

Ministering helpers, they come and they go
At times with a form. At times just a glow.

Yes, coming and going, but please, don't you fear.
There is always at least one angel who's near

Call it a guide, this angel who's yours.
It matters not what you call it; this one you adores.

Give your angel a name, or its light simply feel.
But know in your heart that yes, angels are real.

# May 30

## YOUR SPIRITUAL SPA

Oh, how you do abuse yourself. If you would allow us, we would show you how to treat yourself respectfully and lovingly. We would put you in a sanitarium filled with beautiful flowers where soothing music plays. The air would be fragrant, the temperature not too hot and not too cold. You would lie in a firm yet soft mattress, swathed in soft blankets. And then, two angels would sit beside you, one on each side, and they would spend your waking hours telling you how much you are loved and how worthy you are as they stroke your body and gaze into your eyes. You would be fed fresh fruits, vegetables, and delicious broths. This treatment would continue until you believe the words you are hearing and until the body releases all toxins.

Does such a place exist? You can create exactly such a place, both physical and mental and recover in this spiritual spa. Why have you not done so yet? Do you think you are not worthy?

Begin now to gather the materials and create the surroundings. We will provide the angels. They are waiting in the wings for you to take the first step in loving yourself.

*May 31*

## STANDING STRONG

Sudden shocks shake you like an earthquake. The initial reaction is fright and alarm. You think your world is going to turn upside down. Quickly catch yourself before you fall too deeply into ego's grasp. Recognize how much of your reaction is programmed. "Oh, my God! This is the worst thing that could possibly happen," you are programmed to cry. Is it, or is that a belief from the human side of you?

Fast forward to what you would know as the future and what we know as the unfolding of now-moments. The "future" reveals much growth from these earth-shattering moments. The "future" looks different because life is about change, but you are still here in this so-called future, stronger than ever, having rebuilt your foundation.

Catch yourself before you crumble when the earthquake hits. Do not crumble, but stand firmly upon the foundations of spirit and know that this is yet another test. Are you human or spirit? For now, my friend, you are both.

Lean heavily on that aspect of yourself which is the awakened spirit when all around you seems to crumble, and be the rock. Most important of all, know that you do not stand alone. Your foundation is buttressed by many helpers. Call on them for support and the rock becomes a strong wall, held together with the mortar of love.

# June 1

## TRANSITION

"That is a death sentence!" you think upon hearing of one's illness, as if this is the worst thing in the world. First of all, you cannot know whether healing will take place or not. Mostly, we wish you to examine your belief system.

Yes, those who may be left behind will need to adjust, but death is a welcome transition to some, and a joyous occasion for the soul—a new chapter in the ongoing book of life. It is not to be feared. In fearing death, so many make the last pages of the current chapter frightening and full of low vibrations, instead of a celebration.

What a radical thought change. Grief is very real. We understand this. But perhaps you might view the inescapable transition in a more positive light and help all those around you.

## CHANGING VIEWS

In the valley, all you see are mountains. The climb out appears daunting, but does not the sun shine in from above? It is a beacon, showing you that hope is always there. The valley is not so bad a place to rest for a while.

The mountains stand as symbols of hope, rather than despair. Every journey begins with one step. That step leads to the next, and the next, and before you know it you are climbing higher and higher. There are paths unseen from the bottom … multiple paths, but each one full of possibilities and each one illuminated by the light. Even if you choose to return to the valley for a while, the sun still shines.

The view may change as you go through life with its ups and down, but the sun is always there. Rainclouds and high peaks may obscure its light from time to time, but just as night always turns to day, you too will emerge into the light and be well. All is in perfect order and will show itself to be so when you focus on the Light.

*June 3*

LEAVES

How can something that happens halfway around the planet affect you? Do you not realize that all of you are leaves on the same tree? You all share the same Source. You cannot survive alone. You could not function.

Yes, you think you could go off into a cave and there exist quite happily alone for the rest of your life, but it is God who gives you that life. See God as the Tree itself, not just the trunk and branches and leaves. All of you live and have your very breath in that Tree. What one thinks and does affects all. You may not feel the connection on an individual basis, but how does it affect you when an entire community or an entire nation thinks less than loving thoughts?

How do you raise the vibration of the Tree? It begins with every leaf. You have seen trees die bit by bit of dis-ease, and you have seen trees flourish. Your tree is like a Scientist's experiment. Which way will it go? You are headed in the right direction. Now be a vibrant part of that growth and help the Tree of Life to flourish.

## SANITY

What is sanity? Thinking and behaving as others do, within a set of norms. What happens when one thinks outside of those parameters? "They are off in their own little world," you say, and this is labeled insanity. Most definitely, if one acts and thinks in a way which causes distress or harm to self or others, this is a problem that requires correction. We wish you to understand that often these souls are walking in two worlds at once and cannot discern the difference.

Sanity is best described as balance. In the case of most humans, you are imbalanced ... so fully focused on the human experience that you forget your true home—even now—is in heaven. The heart is the bridge between these two worlds. Find balance by living from the heart, and you will be fully sane.

*June 5*

## FAITH AND TRUST

Does a child understand why you must at times induce pain to ensure its safety? No, it does not. Yet, if it feels your love, it will trust. It is all a matter of trust, perspective, and love.

Those who suffer misfortune do not always see the reasons. We can only ask you to find the love in the situation and to bring love where love is seemingly absent. Many misfortunes occur as a result of the human's free will. We look down upon this and send our love, knowing that misfortune is but a temporary facet of a multi-faceted existence.

Look around you. Love is there. The greater perspective will come at some point, perhaps not whilst still in human form. When it comes— this understanding—you will see and feel the reasons, and you will understand. For now, yes it is challenging, this human life. Faith and trust come by grace.

Do not cease praying for the gifts of trust, patience, and love.

## EARNING YOUR WINGS

Nary a moment passes that you are not loved
Like a hand that strokes the face, velvet-gloved
You feel the soft caress, a breeze that blows
Across the mind, in an instant it shows
That you are never alone, despite your fears.
Love, its magnificent head it rears.
In small ways and great
This is your fate
To discover the Presence in spite of your doubt.
These are what all the tests are about.
These challenges are not just "pass or fail."
It matters not if you rant and rail,
For life is ongoing; there is no end.
These tests are actually a gift we send
To strengthen your trust
Yes, faith is a must
If these trials and tests you wish to survive.
This is the challenge of being alive.
In the end you'll see that this is one book
With a succession of chapters, each one with a "hook."
To rise above is what you learn
And in so doing your wings you earn.
With faith you'll rise, with trust you'll soar.
Through these tests life brings on the way to Heaven's door.

*June 7*

## A TEAM EFFORT

We all work together—those in spirit and those in form. It is a team effort, this thing called Life. Do you think you need a body to exist? Push this thought aside. It is far too Self-limiting.

You are but one aspect of Limitless Power and Love. Love makes the world go round, and love fuels your every action. Team "Love." That is your group identity. You are a player on the team where every position is as vital as the next. Working together, all is possible. Working separately, all is possible as well, but you are never truly separate.

You are as powerful as the next, but oh such joy when you recognize the strength of the team as a whole. Join the team. Recognize a fellow team-member and wink as God winks at you in response.

## UNCEASINGLY

Pray unceasingly. How do you do this? Does this mean that you spend all of your waking moments kneeling with hands clasped? Not at all.

Prayer is an act of communion and acknowledgment of your connection with God—with the Higher Self—and with those on your celestial Team. To pray unceasingly means to acknowledge that you are not alone, to maintain awareness of your connection, and to give thanks for it.

Keep up a running conversation in your mind or merely a silent awareness of the Presence. Why should you do this? Do this and the answer will become clear.

We send you love and blessings and look forward to the communion.

*June 9*

## EYES OF THE SOUL

See into the eyes of the soul. Yes, the physical eyes are a gateway, but so is the heart. You hear the word "see" and immediately think you must gaze with your physical eyes. This is not so. You have eyes of spirit that are not located in the head. They are not shaped like eyes as you know them. We call them eyes only because they are used for perception and lead to greater knowingness.

Seeing with the eyes of the soul means tuning into the heart and the spirit as a whole. Much greater awareness will accompany your every step and breath when you see with new eyes. Realize that you could be physically blind and still see in this way.

Gaze about today with new sight and rejoice in further awakening.

## GRATITUDE

Gratitude goes a long way. It establishes a connection ... taking a conduit that has already been established in your direction and turning it back to the sender. Gratitude closes the loop. This is a circuit of giving and receiving.

What is a circuit, but a never ending loop of gifts. One gives, one receives, and that one gives gratitude in response, and the other receives. Thus you have established a permanent connection, for you now are entangled, as your scientists would explain it.

Spirit is most appreciative when you express gratitude for the gifts in your life. Why? Because you are acknowledging a Source beyond yourself. You are recognizing that you do not stand alone. You are completing the circuit, acknowledging your connection—your oneness—in the grand circle of life. What are you grateful for today? Close your eyes and light up the circuits.

*June 11*

## ONE BITE AT A TIME

You cannot please everyone at all times. There are those who will misinterpret your motives and your meaning and your intentions. Do not fall into the same vibration. Look for the lesson in this encounter. Where two humans interact, there is likely to be imperfection. This is the beauty in relationships. Do you grow defensive when accused, or do you step back and say, "Perhaps I could have done better. Perhaps I did the best I could have done under the circumstances. Perhaps I will change my way of doing things the next time. Thank you for the reminder. May you grow as well from this encounter."

When something causes you anxiety, angst, anger, or anything less than peace, it is always, always an opportunity for growth. The other may not see it as such, and that is not your worry. Grow, grow, grow in peace and love. Correct your thoughts and actions as necessary, thank your teachers, and send love and compassion to self and others. A simple recipe for life, taken one bite at a time.

## NOTHING TO FEAR

You allow yourselves to be frightened by ghosts. You have heard stories from a young age about hauntings and frightening creatures like your boogey man. The heart pounds and adrenaline courses. Some actually enjoy this drama. What are ghosts, but the very same spirit beings as you, except these no longer have a physical body. This is quite a natural state.

All is consciousness, therefore, all spirit is quite conscious. You are aware that you are in a body. The so-called ghosts, however, are not aware that they have left the body, or they do not wish to face this fact. They linger in a place for a while, hoping not to have to move on. They do not like change. They may bang about a bit if change is put in their way. Do you like change? Most likely not. Can you see how some would balk? They do not come nor stay to frighten. They are lost or frightened, or perhaps merely stubborn. As all is spirit/consciousness, you can communicate with them. Open your heart and gently tell them they may move on to a new and far greater experience. Allow them to feel your love, and tell them that far greater love awaits them if they move toward the light.

Does this sound like a silly movie ... like your silly Ghost Busters? This is quite real, but happily, quite rare. You may pass an entire lifetime in human form and never encounter a lost spirit, but there will be one or two who read our words today and find comfort as well as much-needed guidance. For the rest of you, know that when you pass from the physical body you need merely follow the tugging in your heart along the path of bright light and it will lead you directly home.

*June 13*

## PERFECTION

How often do you stop to marvel at the perfection all around you? Why are planets round and not square? Why does a fish have gills? Why does a bear's hair grow thicker in winter? Does the bear need to ask it to do so? Why do your cells divide? Why do the plants and trees give off oxygen? Why is your earth the perfect distance from your sun to support life ... to allow your life?

Why are you here? To enjoy the perfection and to be a part of it.
Do you think it is a random accident that you were born exactly when and where you were and to whom? How could every element of nature be perfectly designed and exclude you?

This is not a world of random acts or designs. Now take your perfection and appreciate it, please. In so doing, you allow that part of you which is always perfect to blossom and let more of that perfection shine through.

## NOT BY CHANCE

Pay attention to signs around you. They are everywhere. These are the Universe's way of speaking to you. Higher Consciousness speaks to you in thought all the time, but you do not hear it or cannot do so through the constant chatter. And so we work with the guides and higher consciousness of others to bring together events that will hit you between the eyes, so to speak.

"What a coincidence!" you cry, and we laugh at your surprise. Had you any idea how much effort goes into orchestrating these planned events that you chalk up to mere chance you would give us far more credit. It is not credit we seek, but your attention. And so we get it in the form of synchronicity.

Do not merely shrug off these attention-getting moments, but stop, turn your eyes skyward and your attention inward, and pass along a bit of acknowledgment and gratitude. It is much appreciated, for in this way you finally acknowledge that we are with you and we are all part of the One.

*June 15*

## WHEN THINGS HEAT UP

Do you fight fire with fire? Perhaps you do. And does it work to put out the original fire? Of course not. It only adds to the conflagration. When anything less than the highest vibration is present, you do not bring in more of the lower vibration. You raise the current vibrations by bringing in more love. It is so very simple, yet so many fail to understand this most basic principle.

When another "gets in your face," as you put it, what happens when you do the same in response? You fan the flames. You have a flare-up. What happens if you release the flow of love, instead? In fact, what if you invite those around you to surround the one who burns with all of your love? Why, the heat will be instantly smothered.

Try it. You will be amazed, and you will laugh at how it took you so long to see how two egos clashing will always produce nothing but sparks, but the ego that is met with a flow of love will cool down instantly.

## GROWING

When you are in new situations, it is easy to practice new ways of thinking. It is the well-worn, familiar experiences which challenge you the most to exhibit your newfound higher thoughts and vibrations.

How do you act around family members and those you have not seen in some time but with whom you have "history"? How do you think and act in old, familiar places? You no longer radiate the same as when you were there and with them in the past, but the memory of how you did lives within the subconscious mind.

Live consciously. Visiting old places and old friends is the perfect time to test if you are, in fact, growing.

*June 17*

## RISE ABOVE

Love is the impetus behind all good deeds. It is fear that is the impetus behind evil. What is fear, but the opposite end of the spectrum of love. Do not fear evil. Bring love into the picture. Radiate such high emanations of love, knowing this is your essence, that anything other than love cannot enter your field.

Fear is a very human emotion. The soul is quite aware of its true nature. It is only being surrounded by those who have fully bought into their humanness that causes others to entrain to that lower vibration. Rise above, my friend. Rise above your human nature to the level of the soul. There you will find no fear, for there you exist as your True Self: Love.

Go forth today as Love in action and see no evil.

## SINGLE-MINDED

Do you see how excitable a dog becomes when it sees its prey? Single-minded focus blocks out all else from its awareness. Can you be the single-minded focus of love? This is the state you want to aim for in meditation to know your true self. Whilst the mind wants to wander, pure consciousness is stillness and focus.

How to achieve this? With intention, desire, and devotion. The more you sit in this state of pure focus, the more you come to know your true state of utter peace and tranquility. There is no need to stay there long in this fully focused state—merely to experience it on a regular basis so that when things become hectic around you, you can return to this sacred place and state at will.

## THE NOW

Some times in your life you must pause
And consider the now, not the cause.
How did you get here matters not as much
As the things around you that now you do touch.

The past is history; the future a mystery
Now is all you have got
So focus here where the action goes on
Or this precious moment is for naught.

## HEAL WITH LOVE

How many times have you turned your head away from an uncomfortable sight? When you see one with a deformity or an infirmity that makes you feel uncomfortable, do you not wince inside and out and turn your head? When you see a beggar on the street, do you look away?

The so-called problem does not go away, for the problem lies in the perception. All is of God. There is naught but love. Remember this when you see something that makes you uncomfortable. You may not understand this expression of the God force. All you can control are your own reactions and your thoughts.

Would it not feel far better to send a blessing in such instances? Instead of looking away, look within your heart. Awaken your compassion and send love. The rays of love are healing, and are felt at a level you may not perceive. Do it anyway. In this way, you help to heal the other, you raise your own vibration, and you help to heal your world. Do this, and the discomfort you previously felt goes away— washed away by the far higher vibrations of love.

*June 21*

## ON MIND READING

You ask how it is possible for one mind to know the thoughts of another. You think this is some kind of magic, as if your mind is jumping across empty space, entering the mind encased inside a physical brain, and reading the inner workings of that physical apparatus. As long as you adhere to this thinking, so-called mind reading, or what is known as telepathy will hold a magical mystery to you.

It is only when you understand that there is no emptiness between your mind and that of another that the magic disappears and logic enters the picture. All is consciousness. There is no beginning and end to consciousness, only a flow ... a spectrum of vibration.

The space between your mind and that of another is merely a ribbon of vibration. Feel the vibration of the ribbon and hear the thoughts, feel the emotions, know the other. It is not magic nor mysticism. It is reality. The reality is: all is One. You are a focus of Infinite Divine Consciousness. What will you do with that understanding?

## HIGHEST, HEALING, AND HELPFUL

Pick a peck of pickled peppers ... how your tongue gets twisted as you say these words, yet you laugh. At times your words get twisted and you do not laugh. At times they come out of your mouth in such a way that you wish you could push them back in.

Words are like that. They can be used to hurt or to heal. We will help you to find the right words if you will learn to pause before speaking. Ask your helpers to give you the highest words, the most healing, helpful words. Ahhhh ... highest, healing, helpful ... do not these words feel much better than biting, bitter bullets?

You have helpers. You are not alone. Call on us, your faithful, forever, friends, and watch with wonder as words wind their way with ease from your lips.

*June 23*

## CONNECTING

Why does stroking the skin feel so good? Why does petting a dog bring such pleasure? What is it about touch that draws you to repeat it? It is all about connection. You touch another, and suddenly there is no separation between you. You become one. Skin and fur are created to feel pleasurable so that you will be drawn to feel this connection. Even the petals of a rose bring you pleasure, for is not a rose a living thing with which you can enjoy connection?

Put your hand on your own cheek and caress it lovingly. How does that feel? If it is not pleasurable, the only reason is a mental association with false beliefs. Now is the time to root them out. Stroke or touch something or someone today that brings you pleasure to remind you of what true connection is. Now repeat the experiment again with the cheek until you feel the same connection.

The pleasure, my friend, stems from love. This is the highest vibration. This is the connection, the vibration all seek. Continue touching. Continue connecting. This is what Life is all about.

## PERCEPTION IS REALITY

Fireworks light up your sky.
You shout and clap in delight.
Such a pleasure you cannot deny,
Yet to some it does bring fright.

They clap their hands upon their ears.
They balk at all the noise.
To some it's joy, to others fear,
And total lack of poise.

Why this difference in how to see,
When both see the self-same thing?
For in your choices all are free.
A fresh interpretation can you bring.

Perception is reality.
This you have been told.
So how will you choose to see your world?
As worthless, or lined with gold?

It matters not what others think,
But how you would perceive.
The choice is always up to you,
In what you do believe.

*June 25*

GIFTS

Share your gifts. What is it you do best? Why do others call them gifts? A gift is something special you give to another with no expectation of anything in return. These abilities and talents which you enjoy are God's gift to you. You could do nothing with them and God would still be most pleased, for your gifts were given to you with no expectation. But gifts, like all things, are meant to be shared for the pleasure and upliftment they bring.

And so, we ask again: What is it you do best? What is it that brings you great joy? How can you use these gifts from God to bring great joy to others? This is where you find your purpose—in expressing your gifts. These treasures need not move mountains or astound others. Your gift may be that you make others smile. Perhaps your gift is in teaching, or perhaps you enjoy creating with your hands, be it food, or art, or beautifully arranged flowers.

You know what it is that brings you joy. Bring that aspect of yourself to the forefront and give freely. This is when joy is found and love does abound.

## REFLECTING THE HIGHEST

All of life is an imitation. What you perceive with the body is merely a reflection of an idea. That which began as thought took on a vibration until it "solidified," in your terms. All retains a specific vibration, and this is how you recognize things—by the consistency of the vibration.

Others recognize you by the consistency of your vibration. As you take on new thoughts, beliefs, and emotions, your vibration changes, at times to the point where others say, "You have changed so much. I no longer recognize you." Your basic vibration as a human remains, but you have molded your energy field with your thoughts and behaviors. Others sense this about you. As you change, you resonate with similar vibrations in others and may no longer resonate with those who have not changed. This oft requires an adjustment in relationships.

You are a reflection of the Creator. All of life is an imitation of how life began as an idea—as a "word." In the beginning was the Word. All is in constant evolution as the word evolves and the vocabulary of creation increases.

What word do you wish to reflect? What aspect of the grand idea do you wish to imitate? Be prepared for changes as you do so, for life is all about change as you go about expressing and reflecting the purest vibration of All That Is.

*June 27*

## HIGHER VIBRATIONS

You crave sweets, those delectable goodies that melt in your mouth. You long for laughter, those belly laughs that leave you with tears running down the face. You stop in your tracks when you see a beautiful sight or hear a perfect tune. You send an email with a touching message or moving picture to all of your friends. Why do you do these things? It is because all of these carry a high vibration. If you understood the energetic nature of the Universe, you would understand why anything less than love and beauty pushes you upward with its lower vibrations toward those that make your heart sing.

The Creator has created for you that most perfect of instruments that resonates in perfect harmony with the higher vibrations and repels the lower so that you know and feel the difference. Be aware of energy. Seek out the higher tones in this song of life, then sing with all your heart using all of your senses in this song that never ends.

## SHINE ON

Shadows of your former self continue to appear. How to banish them?

Shine your light ever brighter. When there is bright light from directly above there can be no shadows around or within you. When you, in turn, shine your light brightly in all directions, you help to dispel the shadows around you. Bear in mind, oh torch bearer, that it is all the same Light. There is only one Source, and it flows through you and as you.

Shine on, oh beacon of Love, and light up your world.

*June 29*

## BRINGING LIGHT

At times you feel insignificant. Do not underestimate your influence. Your very presence can light up a room. Can you think of any better way to make a difference? To bring light where there is darkness ... this is alchemy. You are all on different paths. You all bring different gifts, like leaves upon the same tree—all a bit different, yet all connected, no matter how many branches separate you.

Light up your world today, wherever you find darkness. Help the other leaves to shine and glisten, most especially those who have been in shadow far too long. This is the gift you can bring anywhere, any time. Now, is that insignificant?

## MOST POTENT POTION

Love is the elixir of life—a strong, potent potion that will heal all ills.

Begin with the emotional imbalances such as anger and fear. Have you not thought of this as mental illness? It is quite rampant in your society. How do you cure this illness? Bring in what is missing.

Of course, it is far easier to change the self than others once the intention has been set. Turn up the love. Turn it up full force and it is impossible to feel anger, hatred, and fear.

Radiate your true nature so greatly that soon you begin to have an effect upon others without their even being aware. Now, is that not a potent potion? Ingest it from moment to moment and proceed with your healing.

*July 1*

## AS CLOSE AS YOUR PHONE

You fly in the air in a man-made machine and think nothing of it. What of your ancestors who could not imagine such a thing? The history of your technology is the blink of an eye in the history of mankind. Do you think your ancestors could have imagined a wireless communication device that allows you to talk across great distances instantaneously?

Now propel yourself into the future. Mediums are no longer necessary, for the technology exists to pull the frequency of those who have passed out of thin air and communicate with them in so-called "real time." "Impossible," you say? Can you see cell phone waves? Can you see the television waves? Can you see the spirit-being waves? What is the difference?

All is energy. You merely need learn how to harness it. For now you have very few finely tuned instruments called mediums. Soon you will have one in every household. And then what will your skeptics say? We are sorry, but the world is no longer flat.

## CELEBRATE ALL

Do not look with disdain upon another who has what you want. Be happy for them, instead.

You do not yet realize that they are you in the grander sense. By thinking thoughts of lower vibrations, you lower your vibrations. Send that one love and good will instead. You are in this way blessing yourself as much as you bless them. What you think does indeed come back to you, and so it behooves you to send love to all.

Envy does not become you, nor do you become a more developed soul by surrounding yourself with such thoughts. Celebrate another's success and then you will truly have reason to celebrate.

*July 3*

## WALLS

Let down your walls, those barriers which hold others at arm's length. What if there were no distance between you at all? "Why, then people would know my secrets!" You all have them, these shameful things you know about yourself which you think would keep others from loving you.

Do you think others' secrets are any different from your own? On the other side of their walls are the same little lies: "I am not good enough. I am not worthy. I am no good." And so, you all put up barriers which keep you from discovering the truth.

This truth can only be felt when love flows freely among you, but it begins with yourself, inside your self-imposed barriers. When you have built up enough of this love inside of yourself and around yourself, the walls will come down from the sheer force of it.

## CRYSTAL CLEAR

 Yes, being around lower vibrations can affect you. Be on the lookout for this. Some of you are like sponges and soak up the thoughts and feelings of others.

Regular cleansing is necessary if you are to maintain peace. How do you do this? The recipe remains the same: Deep, cleansing breaths in nature. Visualize the pure energy flowing through you, replacing lower vibrations. Meditate, and focus on the heart and healing.

So many do not realize how much the vibrations of others affect the whole. Those who are empathic realize this quite well. Do your dusting and keep the lens that projects the light inside you crystal clear.

# *July 5*

## HEALTHY CHOICES

Get up off of your couch and stop poisoning your mind. This is not an order or a "should." This is merely a key to raising your vibration. It is your choice how you live your life and how high you wish to vibrate.

You know where some of the lowest vibrations in your current experience come from: that little box you call a television. It spews negative vibrations at the human who remains transfixed and magnetized to it. This apparatus keeps you from developing the very relationships which will raise your vibrations the most. Connections to a box or to another human being? What a choice.

 Isn't life interesting? Will you watch it or live it? We do not wish to take away your fun. There is nothing wrong with entertainment. It is just like food. Moderation is advisable, as is choosing the healthier morsels over those which do you no service. It is always a choice.

## DENTISTRY

You remove a tooth because it hurts. Pain is an indicator that something is amiss. Does the t(r)ooth actually hurt, or is it the nerves around it? Where is your pain really coming from?

Are those around you who you blame for your pain truly the cause of your pain, or is the real cause the nerve endings of your thoughts and beliefs? Pay attention to the pain, then do what you must to extract yourself from the situation. We do not mean for you to run away, merely to change it in some way by changing your thoughts. Then, if action is still required, you will be in a much healthier position to take that action.

Can you play the dentist instead of the one in pain? Step outside of yourself and look down upon the problem as the practitioner with the higher view. "Aha! Here is the root cause, not this surface issue at all." Be your own practitioner, as honest with yourself as you can, then get to work on the root of your pain.

*July 7*

## YOUR SCRIPT

Have we not told you this life is a play? For some it is a drama, for others an adventure. And do you not have your script? You have your role and your words so well memorized, so well-practiced, that you repeat them without thinking.

Perhaps it is time to update your role. Classics are entertaining, but times do change. Can you modernize your lines a bit? How about a bit of improvisation now and then? See how your audience reacts if you change things up a bit. You may surprise yourself. See how it feels to step outside the lines once in a while. Does it bring more peace, love, and joy? Then step to center stage and expound on these new lines a bit more.

You are not stuck in your current role at all. Allow yourself to be inspired. You are a co-creator with the Creative Director of life. Enjoy the freedom.

## GUIDEPOSTS

You have your large billboards that line your highways. These stand out and attract your attention. In the same manner, your life's path is lined with signposts ... guideposts that let you know and give you confirmation that you are going in the right direction. These stand out like beacons, lighting the way. You often see them in the form of great synchronicities. These indeed are indicators that all is flowing well.

Look for the guideposts. Ask to be led down the right path. When just the right person comes into your life, when just the right book falls into your hands, when the heart opens and you have the unexplained desire to laugh or sing, these are guideposts, signs, gleaming billboards that announce to you, "Follow onward, all is well."

# July 9

## IT'S ALL RELATIVE

Are there evil spirits? So many of you believe this is so. Let us start with the basics. Each unit of consciousness—each light-being—has a frequency that is felt and distinguished relative to each other, but all is Spirit. Those of a higher vibration feel more pleasant than those of a lower vibration to the individual. It is all relative. If one unit already vibrates quite low, then another of an equally low vibration would not see the other as evil.

If you are vibrating at a very high rate due to thoughts and actions replete with love, then those units of consciousness which vibrate far, far lower than yours would be felt as a bit of a shock and quite disharmonious. You may label this as "an evil spirit." If you create fear with your own thoughts, you may very well project this as something outside of yourself. This, some of you may label "evil" and give it an identity as "an evil spirit." There is no such thing, for all is consciousness and all is relative.

Your beliefs create your reality. If you believe in evil spirits as a distinct thing, and allow this energy to manifest as fear within your light body, then you instantly lower your own vibration. If you do not allow fear to enter your field of light, then so-called "evil spirits" will not exist to you as something that can harm you. Your only experience will be that of love and a loving universe in which some vibrate higher than others.

Vibrate as high as you are able through your belief only in the One True Power—that of Love—and relatively speaking, you will experience only Love.

## TEAR DOWN THAT WALL!

Defenses. You build them quite solid. Most of all you erect them around the heart. "I am not safe," you feel and so you climb inside the protective barrier you have erected, and it is quite real. Nothing can get in to hurt you, you believe, but nothing can get out as well. There you sit, locked in a world of your making. But the world is not still. Motion is the norm.

Life flows. Love flows, and when you sit behind your defenses, you stagnate. There is no growth. You must be brave if you wish to grow. You must take down the barriers and expose yourself. Yes, bravery results in vulnerability as you expose the tender heart, but in so doing you allow the flow of love in both directions, and in this there is healing.

"Mr. Gorbachev, tear down this wall!" Do you remember this? And the wall came down and there was unity. Child of God, tear down this wall!

Experience the unity—your unity with All That Is, with all that you are … with Love itself.

*July 11*

## GONE FISHIN'

Forgetfulness. Where do the memories go? Are they filed away in a computer? Of sorts, but they are not solid. Thoughts are, indeed, things. They each have their own frequency, and energy cannot be destroyed.

Every thought you have ever had exists as a discreet frequency and is retrievable, but not from the brain ... from the sea of consciousness you are swimming in. Have you forgotten something? Using the power of consciousness, set the intention to retrieve it from the sea. In this way you have cast the hook.

Now, just as in fishing, you need not do anything else. Further casting about merely muddies the waters. Sit still and wait. The bait is set. You may actually leave the line and get on with something else. Because you cast the line with the intention of catching that one specific memory, you will know when it is on the line and can reel in the prize.

Fascinating, is it not? But not magic. Merely the truth of consciousness.

## STRENGTH

The act of surrender seems to you a weakness, when in fact it shows great strength. In saying, "I surrender," you are saying, "I trust that there is something that is greater than I can produce at this moment, and I welcome that assistance."

We are speaking now in a spiritual sense—surrendering to a true Power, not to the false power of two or more egos battling over non-truths. To surrender to a higher spiritual power shows that you know you are connected to and part of something greater and that help is yours for the asking.

All that you are surrendering is the ego, which has no true power in the first place. And so, surrender is part of awakening. Open your eyes to the fact that you are not alone. In so doing, ego has no choice but to take a step to the side.

*July 13*

## WITHOUT CONDITIONS

The ever-present Presence. Do you know it? Yes, you do. You know it as Love. It is there, calling your attention, or you would not seek love in all that you do. But do not seek outside of yourself, for although Love is in all things, it is most reliably in you. You bring forth the Presence, for that is your true nature.

Do you not feel loved enough? Then express more of who you are. Yes, you are loved beyond words at a level you rarely tap into. You can feel this love when you open your heart and set your spirit free.

Do not hold out waiting for others to give their love to you. Awaken. Awaken your very soul and discover there the love you have been seeking. The more you let it out, the more comes back to you. Do you see how very simple it is?

Put no conditions on the soul. It knows only Love.

## "I" VS. "i"

You are beginning to understand this very sacred of concepts, the I AM. When you truly and fully understand yourself as I AM, then you will know that there is nothing but the "I" that sees all, knows all, is all. This is not you. Do not get hung up on your pronouns. Feel this sense of "I" as the one "I" that has no other behind it. Yes, the all-knowing, all-seeing "I" ... the First Cause with all others—all of the little "i's"—being but manifestations of the one I AM.

Once this understanding begins to set in, we ask you to look upon others and see the Great I AM within them. Say not, "That is John and that is Mary." Say instead, "That is 'I'." Do you feel how you rebel? This is because your language pulls you to that place of thinking of the "i" as the ego. Of course you are not John and you are not Mary. But you are an experience of "I," as is John and as is Mary. Set ego aside and see the Great "I" within John and Mary. Feel "I" as the essence of all beings.

Does not John feel the vastness of the "I" within? Does not Mary? The "I" is all that is. Now try again. "I AM That." Look upon John and Mary now and see "I." Say, "I AM That." Now do you understand that what you do and say or do not do and say to another you do unto your Self?

Namaste.

*July 15*

## TEMPTED

Temptations will always surround you. What is a temptation? Something that pulls you like a magnet to do or take something that your intuition tells you is not in your best interest. What is in your best interest? That which increases your loving vibration, your health and harmony, your peace.

Why would you do something that would bring about anything but these pleasant states? At the ego's urging. He convinces you that doing so would bring you greater pleasure, but in the long run, he is usually wrong.

Ego is that little voice which wants you to act against the voice of intuition. He is a greedy fellow. He wants you to stand alone and listen to only him, but in doing so, the end result does not bring peace. When you can learn the difference between ego and spirit—the voice of the soul—you can laugh at temptation and make higher choices.

Once again we advise you to see temptation as ego's voice. Pat him on the head with compassion and understanding, and say, "Thank you for your suggestion, but I choose peace."

## A NEW DAY

Surrender to a Higher Power. This is what your 12-step programs ask you to do, and some have trouble with this concept. To many, a Higher Power carries a negative connotation much akin to a boss. If there is a boss, then that would make the other a subordinate. The ego rebels at this. Ego wants to be the most important—subordinate to no one.

Tell the ego it is special. Tell ego it will always be the only one. Ego likes this, and it is true. There is only one ego for each manifestation of God. But please do not tell ego there is only one Power, and that power emanates from the one and only Source of Love. That power IS love. Ego is a false power. It does not like to surrender, for that act threatens its very existence.

Surrender to Love and discover that ego has no power. When you surrender to love, there is no longer a need for separation; there is no longer a need for ego. It does not take 12 steps to return to love. There is only one step. Step over ego, but do it gently, for ego has served you well. But ego's day has passed. It is a new day, and your time has come.

*July 17*

## THE LOW HANGING FRUIT

The fruit on the branches hangs low—so low you can pluck it with no struggle. "Low hanging fruit"—an expression you have for those things in life which are easy to harvest and well at hand. God is like that—there all around you waiting to be harvested. This may sound strange to you if you see God only as a being in human form. If this is so, you are missing the low-hanging fruit.

Reach out and pluck a cherry, a peach, an apple, a pear. God is there. Pet a puppy, smell a flower. God is there. View the sunrise, marvel at the stars. God is there. God is all that you see—not limited like the human being. Form and formless, shape and shapeless, in every crack and cranny, in every empty space. There is nowhere that God is not. In every cell? Yes, indeed. In every breath you take, every step you make, every thought you create.

Reach out and touch the face of God in one you love today. Take your hand and caress your own face. God is Love, and now you are expressing your Godliness. You do so every time you kiss, laugh, speak, and cry. May they be tears of joy. If not, know that God cries with you as you grow and learn together ... as One, ripening on the vine in the sunshine of God's love.

## LESSONS

You think that others are your greatest challenge—dealing with less than ideal situations and less than the highest vibrations. Do you not yet see that others have nothing to do with your own low vibrations? They are aids to your growth, tools to help you in your soul's advancement.

Do you grow impatient with others for you think they are impeding your spiritual growth? Then, impatience is your lesson! Do you grow easily frustrated and out of sorts? It is quite easy to blame another. Look first to yourself, and then, most importantly, have patience with yourself. Laugh with us with a large dose of love as you realize that you have not reached perfection yet.

We love you. Please do the same.

*July 19*

## BOOKENDS

When your world becomes hectic and crazed, you forget easily who you are. You slip into doing-mode instead of being-mode. Who is doing the doing? Are you acting alone? When your life becomes crazed, it becomes far too easy for you to believe that you are.

Ideally, you would remember to check in with Spirit frequently throughout your day. In human form this often falls by the wayside. Book-end your days then with a deliberate period of communion, be it in prayer or meditation or both. This will be time well spent.

There is no need to rush about feeling harried. Stop, take a breath, and connect. This is the secret to balance.

## NEW CLOTHES

Throw away your childish toys which no longer serve you, for you have grown. They no longer hold interest. It is time to move on. And so it goes as you progress along the path of wisdom as well.

That which you once thought was interesting now appears foolish. Why is this? You are vibrating at a higher frequency now. Humor that makes fun of others reveals itself as hurtful. Humans hurting other humans hurts you. In a way, are these not childish games as well? Yes, when viewed as a young soul versus one which has awakened a bit more.

Be patient with yourself as you grow, but remain alert for signs of change as you outgrow your clothes one by one and grow into a whole new way of being.

*July 21*

## HELP IS HERE

What can you say to one who is hurting so badly?

Often, what will help the most is "I am here," and then be sure that you are there. Hold a hand. Wipe a tear. Talk of whatever they wish, or simply listen. Whilst in their presence, or even if not, send waves of love. Visualize them surrounded by a shaft of healing light. In this way you give them strength.

You are the presence of comfort, the very presence of strength. Are these not the things all people pray for? You are that in physical form.

You are a God-send. How can you fulfill your purpose today?

## SOFT VOICES

When it is so quiet that you can hear a pin drop, then you could actually hear a choir of angels sing. Your brain shields you from the many voices passing through your energy field, and this is a very good thing, for there is nothing but energy all around you and passing through you.

When you do hear a voice in your head, we can help you to sort out which voice is worth listening to. Listen to your body when the message flits through the mind so quickly and softly that you are not quite sure you heard it. How did that message feel? Was it Truth? If you are not sure, wait until you are in a place where you truly could hear a pin drop. Calm the human mind with a few deep breaths, and ask for clarity. "Was I making that up?" you may ask about the original message. "What are You trying to tell me?"

In this way of believing that there is a Source of wisdom speaking to you, and then having the intention of hearing the Answers, you open the communication circuits. The final element is trust. Belief, intention, and trust—the triad of truly hearing.

*July 23*

## THE GREATEST POWER

A great cliff drops straight down, and yet you stand at the edge of it. You trust that you will not fall. Why is this? You are relying on the laws of the natural world to keep you safe—the law of gravity, the law of balance.

What do you know of the spiritual laws? They are even stronger. The greatest of these is the Law of Love, for it governs all that is. Love overcomes hatred, anger, and evil, for these have no power of their own.

Your scientists do not know what gravity is, yet they know how to use it and how to overcome it for their advantage. How many know how powerful love truly is? It can, indeed, move mountains, if you would only use it. It exists in every place, in every being, in every thing, for love is All That Is.

Love shaped the mountains just as love shaped you. You hold within your every cell, within your very consciousness the most powerful essence that is.

How will you use that power today?

## THAT PLACE CALLED "NOWHERE"

Look into another's eyes and there behold the soul--
That part of you that's always whole.
The soul it knows no judgment; the soul knows only love,
Connected as it is to all above.

You think you are so limited,
That human life is all there is.
But when you gaze within the eyes,
You know where "nowhere" is.

"Nowhere" is that place of being
Where time and space are not ...
A place that in the human form
A part of you forgot.

It's from this place of "nowhere"
That spirit does arise.
A place of love, pure consciousness,
Far more glorious than the skies.

You long for it, for it's your home--
That "nowhere" place that's yours.
Call it heaven if you will,
Then step beyond its doors.

*July 25*

## WITH GENTLE CORRECTIONS

Blessed be the meek, and blessed be the mighty. Always you try to categorize the human—to place labels dependent upon characteristics. There is no one Being who judges one human against another.

The soul only judges itself. You become quite skilled at this whilst in human form, but when you shed the skin the judgment of self by the self is with only love. Yes, there is regret when the soul recognizes lost opportunities to love, but it is not the critical, biting, hurting judgment that you know now. Be easy on yourself and others now, as the spirit is.

All are truly blessed, for all are spirit. As such, there is nothing to judge, merely to observe and to gently correct when higher choices can be made.

## PLAYING GOD

So often others do not do as you wish. This to you is frustrating. It is frustrating for you are playing God. You think you have the big picture. Yes, it is true, you are all interconnected, all working for the greater good of the whole, but does a heart cell control a liver cell? Does a brain cell try to tell a skin cell what to do? Each has its own role. Each contributes to the whole.

Yes, it is important to each cell that the other thrive, but they do mind their own business. There is higher consciousness running the heart, the liver, the brain, and the skin, and yet an even higher consciousness running the whole show.

You become frustrated when others do not do what you envision they should do, either for their benefit or yours. Can you find it in yourself to trust that there is a higher consciousness running your show and simply do your best in your role right now? Life will flow as it is supposed to if you will but let it.

*July 27*

## REPAIR THE BONDS

Step-son, step-daughter, step-parents and the like. This is a new form of relationship, formed not of blood, but of a bond—a bond of marriage. Yes, it is true there is no blood relation, but do you think it is an accident they are in your life?

Imagine the moment before all were born and the decision was made to help each other to learn in some way. It was decided to be a step closer than most by the legal bond of marriage, a step farther away than blood relatives, but a step forward in your growth caused by this bond.

As with all of your interconnections, your "steps" afford you great challenges, which we wish you to see as opportunities. You chose each other. Trust us in this. If the bond now is not fully loving, know that at one time, in a different dimension it was.

Ask for guidance to know what you can do to return to that relationship. That will be a step in the right direction.

## WORKING TOGETHER

Give credit where credit is due,
And remember: It is not always you.

With these short poetic lines we wish you to know that you rarely act alone. Yes, you strike out and use your free will constantly, but does that mean that you are actually free?

God is your very being. You are God-breathed. It is God that giveth and God that taketh away. Yet, you are free to make choices. In this way you grow, just as a child does. Ego will get you in trouble. Ego wants to strike out on its own all the time. Such impudence!

Be grateful for your guides, who ensure that you are never alone, in spite of what ego may tell you. Even if you are not aware of their existence they keep you straight. Like a parent who will let you earn a few bumps and bruises but will make sure you avoid the truly big falls, your guides are always there. You are part of a very big team. It may seem to be made of separate players, assistant coaches, and the Head Coach, but in reality, there is just the One.

Give credit where it is due.

## NEVER LOSE SIGHT

"I of myself do nothing." Never forget these words and you have passed the test.

The moment you begin to take credit for what you think are your works, you have lost sight of Truth. This is why it is so very important to maintain your connection with Spirit on a daily, if not moment-to-moment basis whilst in human form. Walking amongst other humans it is far too easy to slip back into allowing ego to run the show. You are not the ego. You never have been.

It is when that shell first cracked and your light began to shine outward from within and onto others that you were truly reborn. It was through that connection with your true Spirit that your life as an awakened spirit truly began.

Never lose sight of that now that your sight has been regained.

## GOOD VIBRATIONS

Why does the human turn to alcohol or drugs? So as not to feel the lower vibrations of being human. This we understand. It is a temporary break from being human, but it is moving in the opposite direction from Spirit.

You have heard many songs about a natural high. Being in nature, breathing in fresh air can bring a great rise in personal vibrations that are moving closer to the vibration of Spirit rather than away. Rest assured, all is God, but Spirit is felt more clearly at the higher end of the spectrum.

Breathe in the fresh air and pull Spirit into your lungs. Yes, get off the couch when you do not feel like it. Take a walk in nature. Commune with Spirit and clear your human head.

*July 31*

## SEEING SPIRIT

It is quite easy for the human to judge another, for the human is ruled by ego. The spirit is not ruled at all—it simply is one with the Great Spirit. It knows only oneness and hence it knows only love.

There is a reason for your humanity. You exist in human form to experience life in all of its diversity, complexity, and beauty. It is only when you forget your true nature as spirit that this experience of diversity becomes one of criticism versus one of observation and appreciation. When there is harshness in the judgment, your human side is dominant. When there is compassion and love, Spirit is at the fore.

We look upon you with naught but love, even if you may from time to time be oh so very human. That is truly why you are here—to develop the Spirit side of you to such a point that you see the Spirit in all others and appreciate when others are merely being human. It is at that point that you will no longer feel the need to judge and will send only love.

## HIGH OR LOW?

When challenges come, do not some face them with a smile and others a frown? Is either right or wrong? Of course not, but the one with a smile will meet with an easier time, for they are bringing unto themselves higher vibrations, allowing the Life Force to flow more freely. With this comes a feeling of greater vitality and a sense of connectedness.

You are always connected to the Source, and your angels are always at your side, but when you surround yourself with thoughts of a higher vibration, it is far easier to sense your guides and helpers. No path is right or wrong. We are at your side through thick and thin, no matter what. It is you who creates the high or low vibrations in your field, however. What will you create today?

*August 2*

## STRETCH AND BEND

Stand your ground if you will, but which is more likely to survive the storm: the tree which bends or the one that is rigid?

Growth entails stretching and bending. You do not become a tall, wise tree without bending quite a bit along the way. There is only one view when you remain rigid. When you bend you see many sights on the way down and back up. Now you are free to choose, having gained a bit of insight along the way.

With insight comes wisdom. Why do you think they call it a "wise" old tree? It has done quite a bit of bending along the way. Stand your ground if you will, but be willing to bend. There is no dishonor in this. There is no shame.

The one who bends learns far more, is more open, and receives the greatest gifts.

## AS A CHILD

Your sacred writings tell you to be as a child. There is great wisdom in this. Let us examine why. It is because of this very reason! The adult examines everything, dissects things, and then worries about them ... sees the flaws in them, sees the impossibility, sees the limitation, and sees the potential for failure.

Now let us not examine it. Let us simply be childlike. Let us play. Let us rejoice. Let us laugh and spin about for no reason whatsoever, with no explanation other than that it feels good.

Joyful. Is this not how the Creator wishes to enjoy its creation? Be as the child: full of joy, curiosity, and unbridled love for all things. You have learned to be an adult by watching adults. As a child you wanted nothing more than to be grown up. Now that you are there, it is okay now to regress for a while and remember your true nature as a free spirit.

*August 4*

## PERFECTLY IMPERFECT

Zero defects. Yes, again we bring this up, because again you are striving for perfection. To make no errors is a laudable goal, but it leads to fear and frustration. Can you just be happy "being"? Can you just enjoy the game for what it is?

All of life is about the experience and how you grow from it. The lessons you take with you add to the Whole. If all of you were perfect all of the time, where would be the learning? It is how you handle the imperfections that brings the most growth.

Embrace your so-called defects. See and love the imperfections for what they are—part of the perfection that is you.

## WHOOSH

Scurry, scurry. Why so much rushing about? Where are you going in such a hurry? Do you even know where you are? Stop for a moment and look around. How did you get here? Do you remember? Be present and you will discover a whole new world—one which has been rushing past as you focus always on the future.

There are those around you who would love for you to take a breath. Your soul would like to say hello and get to know you, but that requires catching your breath. Try it. You may be surprised at what you have been missing.

*August 6*

## CYCLES AND CIRCLES

Circular movements represent the shape of creation. All arises from the void and returns again to silence. All is vibration. You arose from the mind of the Divine Mind, beginning as pure spirit and to Spirit you will return. You experience what you know as birth and death, but these are merely re-cycling of the spirit into a form which can undergo experience.

Do you see the origin of this word "re-cycle"? Look at nature, and there you will see countless cycles. All is cyclical in a world without end. This is why you can take comfort in the phrase, "This too shall pass."

There will always be sunshine after the rain. Yes, this means the rains will come again as well, but understanding the nature of cycles and your nature as a spirit-being, you can ride the wave in peace.

## AWAKE AND CELEBRATE

Oh, how you do disdain the physical body! "It is too large … It pains me here, and here, and here … This does not work right … This does not look right …" Paradoxically, your complaints oft become even worse as you begin to awaken to your true nature as a spirit-being. You place your focus on the spirit body and see the physical body as an instrument. This is true. A most perfect tool it is for expressing Spirit, but do you not see that the body is Spirit as well?

Have you not learned that God is All That Is? Then, is not the body comprised of Source Energy as well? Yes! And so, does it not make sense to revere every cell of your body? To honor every feature? To give thanks for this divine instrument, no matter how it looks or how it may seem to fail you? Do you see now how your human perceptions fail you, instead?

Yes, you are an awakening spirit-being, but until you can look upon the physical body as every bit as holy as the spirit-body and honor both with equal reverence, then you still slumber a bit. This is fine. Do not use your sleepiness as yet another reason to berate your humanity. This life experience is all about the journey of awakening.

On this day of awakening, celebrate the body with its perfection and imperfections, for that is life in the physical world. For this you have a physical body, so raise your physical arms to the sky and use your physical voice to celebrate and give thanks.

*August 8*

## OPEN

Miracles happen when you get out of the way. What do we mean by this? You have your preconceived notions of how the world works. These expectations create your reality. If you do not believe in Santa Claus, you may very well receive lumps of coal.

Open your mind to possibilities beyond your imagining, to experiences no other has yet had, and then prepare yourself. A jolly being with a white beard may very well put a special gift right in your lap.

The miracles reveal themselves when you surrender fixed images of how your world works.

## EARTHBOUND

What are ghosts?

The lingering vibration of those who do not yet want to fully embrace the experience of no longer being in human form. They resist going fully to the light, and thus retain a bit more of the human vibration than that of pure spirit.

There is nothing to fear. This more earthly vibration makes them visible and detectable by those who would not normally see or hear those not in human form. You can help such beings by suggesting that they move on. Now that they are in spirit, they will have a far greater experience if they move toward the light.

As for you, you are still in human form, therefore there is a reason you are still earthbound. You have more to experience here. Move toward the light in your heart and make this earthly time all the more enjoyable.

*August 10*

## THE DRIVING FORCE

"Love makes the world go 'round." These again are some of your lyrics to a well-known song, but yes, they have a literal meaning. It is Love indeed that is the creative impulse of the universe and all universes beyond it. Were it not for Love, the world as you know it would implode and darkness would prevail.

Your world—the one in which you are the center of your own universe, the sun of your own solar system—consists of you surrounded by the planets of your family and friends. It is Love which makes you shine and revolve and yes, breathe. Breathe in more of it, would you.

When you feel as if your life may just implode, step out of your little universe and rise above it all. See the bigger picture, where chaos has no place, where Love is the one guiding Force and Source, and get back into alignment.

Your trajectory may wobble a bit now and then, but the course and path you are on is quite clear and stable … ever onward, ever upward, and moving ever so surely in the direction of, and under the direction of, Love.

## MIRACLES ALL AROUND

Miracles are all around you when you have eyes to see and ears to hear. Miracles big and small are signs of the interaction of two worlds, two realities.

When you have faith, or better yet the knowingness that other dimension exist beyond your own, miracles become the norm. Still, you celebrate them as we do also to see that you are paying attention. Pay attention. The signs are all around you.

A miracle is not magic, but a mirror of the state of awareness in which you find yourself. Ask to behold miracles in your life and they will become the norm – a reflection of the openness of your mind and spirit.

*August 12*

## FEARLESS

Can you live fearlessly? How badly do you want to?

Fearless living requires first and foremost understanding you are spirit first and foremost and that that aspect of you which is spirit cannot be harmed. It lives on forever. No bullets, no arrows, no words, no knives, no car accidents, no falls, no wounds, physical or emotional, can harm it.

Then you must identify the programmed messages which speak contrary to the Truth that you have planted at both the conscious and subconscious level that you continue to tell yourself. As you find these, release them and replace them with powerful, loving words which speak to the Truth of who you are.

Fearlessness is a state of mind which becomes a state of being through practice.

## AT HOME

Settle back in your favored place--a place where you feel at home and safe. Why do you feel so there? For you are warm and comfortable. You know that nothing can bother you there.

This place you have chosen exists in the physical world, but such a place exists within the soul as well. Your sanctuary. Go there often. You may be experiencing chaos externally, but by merely closing the eyes and breathing deeply, you can return for a moment or more to this home that is always there.

You cannot stay there forever whilst enjoying the human experience, for that would defeat the purpose of having your human experience, but go there just often enough and as needed to remind you what is truly Real. You are always safe and loved.

## THE PICTURE

You are not autonomous.  Thank God.
You do not act alone.  Thank God.
You need not fear.  You have help.
Thank God.
When things go well, thank God.
When things get out of hand, call on God.
Are you beginning to get the picture?
You are loved.  Thank God.

## ABUNDANCE

Cornucopia ... abundance ... it does not always come at once, and it may not last. All things come and go, ebb and flow. Does that mean you give up? No, you press on, knowing that abundance is your true nature.

As spirit, you have everything you need. Love is abundant, but you shut it off when you experience the ebb of human life. You control the flow of love and gratitude. All else flows from this.

When what you desire as a human dries up, open the flood gates of gratitude and let the love flow abundantly. The tide will come back in. It is the Law of Life and of Rhythm.

*August 16*

## ON PURPOSE

Into every life come challenges. Were it not so, there would be no point in being human. How you handle them is the test—the test of being human.

You cannot stay here forever. The human body is a beautiful instrument, but it does break down. At times this is intentional, caused by poor choices; at others, merely the aging of the machine. Before it gives out on you, you may want to use it for the purpose for which it was designed. It houses and expresses the most beautiful treasure of all—the spirit that is you.

Treat this vessel with love and respect. You have a lot more learning to do.

## JUST THINKING . . .

If you are filled with strife, you are thinking like a human. If you are filled with fear or anger, you are thinking like a human. You will always think, for you are consciousness incarnate, but you are also consciousness discarnate, and that is the part of you that feels no fear, no anger, and no discord.

Would you like to experience such a state without leaving this bodily experience? Shift your focus and place the intention. Now step outside the box you have placed yourself in. How did you do that? By thinking.

Do you get it yet? Peace is only a thought away.

*August 18*

## WHAT DO YOU EXPECT?

Expectations … they follow a spectrum from high to low, from beyond the stars to none at all. From whence come these hopes and dreams or lack thereof? All come from a seed of an idea. All arise from the mind, and there they are left to you to grow. Even if you have no expectations, the seed is still there, or you would not be aware of the lack. Is this not so?

How will you choose to nurture your ideas? Expectations go hand in hand with belief. If you think you can, you can. It is that simple. If you have no expectations, it is quite likely the seed will never sprout.

Expectations are fed by your own mind, yes, but do you not also allow others to feed them? Be aware always of your thoughts. How high can you raise your expectations? Why, there is no limit, for you, like your Creator, have no bounds. Consciousness is infinite.

Reach for the sky, and then soar beyond it.

## IMMERSED

Countless times you have cried out, "Oh, God, help me!" You do so when you feel utterly alone and powerless, when you are in pain, or facing some great challenge. You do so knowing intuitively that you are not alone, or you would not cry out at all.

It is true. You are never alone. If you knew how truly loved and surrounded by Spirit you are, you would never experience this word you call "lonely." God is there when you feel no need for crying. You are immersed in God's love. You breathe because this Love animates you.

So cry out, if you must, but God knows when you need assistance. If it helps you to remember, then cry loudly. But at other times fail not to whisper softly, "Thank you for this gift of life. May I use it wisely, and may thy will be done."

*August 20*

## CHECK THE FILTER

How deceptive is the physical body!

Do you not judge a book by its cover more often than not? In many cases it is an accurate indicator of what thoughts and emotions lie inside another, but not always. Apply the same test to yourself. What would people think if they judged you at first glance? The outside wrapper of all of you hides a treasure beyond measure.

Only the heart is a worthy interpreter of what lies inside. Be cautious of allowing any of your physical senses to interpret your world. Only the soul knows what is real, and reality filtered through a human brain will always be suspect.

## MAGNIFICENT YOU

Magnificence. That is what you are. Do you not yet realize this? Why are you drawn to a magnificent view, a magnificent mountain ... magnificence of any kind? It is because like attracts like. You came from Magnificence. Magnificence is all there is, trying so very hard to express itself.

Anything that you observe or experience that is less than the full expression of Magnificence is illusion. That is why so many enlightened ones speak of the human experience as illusion. So many walk about deluded, thinking they are less than Magnificence, and that becomes their reality.

Rise up, above the illusion and false perceptions. Find and see the Magnificence all around you, then act in accordance with your true nature, and you will be bringing reality to illusion. Now, substitute the word "God" for Magnificence and bring a bit more understanding to your concept of God.

You are Magnificence expressing itself, nothing less, but oh, so much more than you imagined.

## LIFE EXPECTATIONS

What is your life expectancy? Eighty years? Ninety? One hundred? If so, then you are cheating yourself. Your life expectancy is now, followed by now, followed by now, and now, and yet another now-moment.

There will come a moment when the world outside of your sense of I AM makes a rapid shift from one state of awareness to another as you take a very short trip from the physical world as you now know it to yet another very solid existence that you will know as soon as you are in it. Other than the change in perspective, and--oh yes--the overwhelming awareness of the presence of love, life will go on.

So what is your life expectancy? Not eighty or ninety or one hundred anything, but an infinite number of love-filled nows.

## CHOICES

A fly is an irritant to you. It carries disease, you have been told. Then why does it exist at all? Each creature on earth serves a purpose, or it would not exist. You swat the fly or shoo it away. Do others do the same to you, seeing you as an irritant?

You serve a purpose as well. Billions of humans walk the earth, and each of them serves a purpose, or they would not be here. You are part of the miracle of Life—one of the chosen to be here as a human instead of as a fly. So highly evolved are you that you can reason and make choices that a fly, or a horse, or dog cannot.

All creatures have the capacity to love. Only the human makes the choice to give or withhold love. Only the human makes a choice to be a deliberate irritant. How very lucky you are. Will you spread your wings today and fly or be an irritant? The next time you see a fly, thank it for the lesson.

*August 24*

## ADAPTATION

When those around you change beyond recognition, you change as well. It is human to want everything to stay the same, but every cell in your body is constantly changing, as is every vibration of your spirit body.

Change propels the soul ever onward in its quest for growth. Do not fight it. Adapt. Do you not see the most beautiful evidence of adaptation in nature? Look at the insects that change their shell to match the external environment and blend in. This is for their survival. To better survive this earthly experience, accept change as a constant.

Allow your "skin" to change colors as things around you change and ever easier will be the journey.

## HOME

Home is where the heart is.  This is true.  Home lies within you.  It is not a physical place that you go, but a nexus of emotions, the primary one being comfort-love.

The locus of this feeling lies adjacent to the physical heart.  You can rest your consciousness in this point of love at any time and thus "go home."  So, indeed, home—within your physical body—is where the heart is.  It is also where your friends and loved ones gather, for do they not engender an upwelling of love in the heart area?

Go home now, without ever moving the physical body.  Move the part of you that never dies to the locus of love that is always within you, and go home.

*August 26*

## A MORE PEACEFUL VIEWPOINT

Do you know where those who act from ego come from? A place of fear. Their actions may seem like confidence, but inside there is the fear that they will not be loved or will not have or get enough of what they think they need to survive.

Do not look with disdain upon those who act with excessive pride or arrogance. See them, instead, with compassion, for inside they are as frightened children. Send them love and silent blessings.

May you never fear. May you never lack for love. If you find yourself thinking from a place of lack or fear, may you recognize that this is ego and not the real you.

## CORDS

Dearest children, you are so very loved. Love does go, indeed, beyond words. The greatest love cannot be expressed in words, only felt. And this is the beauty of love. You need no words to express it, no hands to pass it along. You need only the mind to move it.

Concentrate on the heart area, the locus of love. Allow it to build until it threatens to burst from your chest, and then choose a target. This may be one who stands before you. It may be one or a group out of sight, or it may be all of God's creation. Holding that recipient in mind, send it forth, your love. Be fairly warned, however, that this love you send out never leaves you completely.

Once you send your love with intention, the connection remains like a cord. Can you imagine if you send your love to the world with intention on a regular basis? Well, then, you could not help but feel the oneness, could you?

Think about that.

*August 28*

## STEPS

In this lifetime you will travel many miles, but the most important step is the one you take right now, for each builds upon the other. Your steps lead you to a place you cannot anticipate now, for you have not the big picture.

Worry not. When each step is fully guided and not taken haphazardly, the path unfolds beautifully. Each step behind you has led you to this moment. Are you unhappy with this moment? Change your course.

Do you not know which direction to turn? Ask. Attune. Be receptive to the guidance that is always there. Again we say, worry not about 100 steps from now. If you attune now to the Guidance within, each step will be perfectly placed.

## POLLYANNA

The Pollyanna Show. A good title for a program that all should take part in daily. What is a Pollyanna, but one who sees all clouds as white, one who greets all with a loving smile, one who is eternally joyful and full of peace. Such a one is viewed as naïve in your world—innocent to the point of being laughable. And so, you shy away from being the Pollyanna who sees only goodness and light. Instead, you buy into the less than good things you see about you. You do not realize that in allowing yourself to see the "evil," you are perpetuating it. "Oh!" You recoil. "I cannot take responsibility for another's actions!" But oh, my children, you can. You are all one and the same energy. What you send out comes back to you.

See and be only goodness, and that is your experience. Believe that naught but goodness exists, and that very thought allows goodness to perpetuate. Consciousness creates reality. By buying into the mass consciousness, you are allowing mass destruction to occur. We apologize if this sounds harsh. Of course you cannot personally take responsibility for those things that happen halfway across the world.

Or can you?

You, as an individual focus of Love are part of the whole. One ray of light can brighten a room. Billions of rays can banish the darkness forever. Yes, of course, you cannot heal the world, but you can bring in the light instead of perpetuating the darkness. Be a Pollyanna and participate in The Pollyanna Show. It is far better than the alternatives. Heal your world one soul at a time. Begin with your own soul by spreading light instead of acknowledging the darkness.

*August 30*

## THIS ONE

"This One" – this one incarnation you are experiencing – this is what others would know as "you" and what you would know as "I." This One thinks it is the center of the universe, even though there are billions of This Ones. And so, This One takes on a name, a unique name to identify this go-around of soul-force, of God Energy.

You, as This One, once affixed with a label such as Mary Smith or John Jones become ever more differentiated. This One takes on a personality, warts and all. The little quirks of This One are at times laughable and at other times annoying. There is great genius in having billions of This Ones experiencing life in physical form. This gives the soul a chance to work out the kinks, to smooth out the bumps caused by other This Ones' experiences in this vast, ongoing exchange of energy. Hopefully, This One will do a lot of smoothing out and return to the fold quite a bit smoother this one time.

You, as This One this time, are here to help the God-Energy to grow ever more fine and evolved. You, as This One this time, play a vital role in adding to the whole, for even though you may seem separate, you are merely having a This One experience for a time in the world of time. Do not become so attached to the label of Mary Smith or John Jones that you forget This One great lesson.

## NOISE

Turn down the noise. We are trying to talk to you. Your higher self is trying to whisper in your ear, but you cannot hear it through the din. Ego tells you to turn up the volume. Turn on the television and the radio. Put your earbuds in so that you do not have to think and, heaven forbid, you do not have to feel. If you did that, your soul would start to heal. You would no longer identify with ego and allow him to have his way.

Silence during meditation is far more beneficial than you know. Silence at regular periods throughout your day is transformational.

You become restless and afraid when it is "too quiet." Why is this so? For then you start to feel the lower vibrations that still need healing. To heal them, they must first be felt and then brought fully to the light. When the radio and television blare, ego is quite happy, for you do not hear the quiet voices.

It is your choice. Listen, feel, and heal, or remain a slave. There is no right or wrong, no easy way or hard way, simply a new way of being that we offer you to try and see how it feels to be silent.

*September 1*

## NOTHING TO DREAD

What is dread, but fear? What is fear, but a perception? Fear is a very human characteristic. One who knows themself as spirit first and foremost knows peace—knows that there truly is no death. It is your attachments that hold you in fear and fill you with dread. If you had no attachments, there would be nothing to lose. Without loss there is nothing to fear, nothing to dread.

Life is eternal. You are an expression of Life. You may temporarily be out of sight of those you love, but never do you lose them or they you. Fear not. Be not filled with dread. Take a break from being human regularly and fill yourself with the certainty that God IS, and you are That.

That is all you need to know.

## WITH EASE

There is no need to try so hard. No need to struggle.

When has trying ever gotten you exactly what you wanted every time? Yes, of course you have had success from trying and from hard work, but that is quite different from struggling. Hard work can be done with mental ease. In that way, hard work can be mentally effortless.

Surrender. Become your own ally. Know that you need not struggle, for you are being helped and guided in every moment. Know that when you cry out, "Oh, God, why isn't this working?!" that your angst is a sign that you have not surrendered. Know that one day you will see the big picture and see how every moment was a lesson given to you by your choosing at a higher level. You will see then that all struggling was in vain. If you had surrendered and realized that all was in perfect order, you would have learned the lesson and grown in any case with far more ease.

*September 3*

## FROM UP HIGH

All the world's a stage upon which you dance and act. You fancy yourself the star, stepping into center stage and waiting for the spot light to illuminate you for all to see. All of the other actors rotate around you. The sets and scenes come and go, but do you not see that the stage and play is just a bit different for each player? How can all of you be the star? How can all of you take center stage? It is because there is not just one drama, but limitless ones, all playing out in the Mind of the one Great Director.

When the drama gets to be too much, it is because you are only seeing life from one of limitless dramas at the center of the action. So as to not become overwhelmed or overblown with self-importance, allow the Stage Manager to lift you up high from a set of invisible wires. From here, what do you see? Lo! Billions of other stages! The actors jump from stage to stage, interacting, and they all revolve, these stages, with none of them at the center at all!

The pressure is off. You do not have to be the star, nor the head victim. The light shines on all of you at once. You are all supporting actors, supporting each other. No stress. No worries. Have fun. Enjoy the drama, knowing you can rise above at any time and see through the eyes of your Co-Creator.

## REACH OUT *

When a person takes their own life, they are merely detaching consciousness from form. It is impossible to take away Life. It is God who giveth and God who taketh away. The human merely makes choices through the exercise of free will. In this way, the human helps the soul to evolve.

The early departure from the school of human life by choice does nothing to help the soul evolve and is deleterious to the growth of the Whole. There is no judgment nor punishment, merely recognition that no growth has taken place and that human pain has resulted for those still in human form.

Think twice, think thrice, and think again before making a choice that is permanent to the current human form. Such a choice does not end suffering. Resort to prayer--constant prayer—with the knowing that you are contacting a Source which will send help.

You are not alone. You never have been. You exist for a reason. You need not suffer. The light is there, and one will be sent to you to lead you from the darkness. Trust in this as you pray. Reach out.

*\*Note from Suzanne: When Sanaya shared this message they stated that the message was meant for "one who will read these words and needs to hear them". I include it and a similar message on the next page because there may be one who needs to read these words at this time. For others it may provide answers you seek.*

*September 5*

## YOU ARE NOT ALONE*

Suicide. Not an uplifting thought. Some call it "a permanent solution to a temporary problem." We call it "death by ego." It is only when the self believes itself to be separate and alone and the source of its own power that it gives itself permission to transition early and abort this earthly experience. Yes, abort. Suicide is self-abortion. Heavy topics, but please bear with us, for there is one who will read these words today who needs to know that while suicide is an option, there are far better choices to be made.

Even in the depths of despair, God is there. Love is there. You are not alone. This sense of great desperation is nothing but a sign that you have lost your way a bit. Turn around and take the hand of the nearest human. They have been sent to guide you. Know that your God and your angels and guides have not forsaken you, only that your own grief is barring you from feeling their presence.

Do not cease praying. This maintains the connection, and the way will be shown to the Light within. Suicide is not a permanent solution, for life is eternal. Sooner or later all must learn the lessons of life, difficult as they may be. Suicide is but a temporary escape ... delayed gratification. Be brave. Find the love here on your earthly plane whilst here and know gratification and love beyond words. It awaits you here on earth. Trust in this and simply hold in your heart the knowledge that love is your birthright.

You will emerge from this temporary darkness far stronger, here and now. You are not alone.

*See note on September 4

## THE "I" OF THE STORM

Amidst the chaos there is peace. Is this not the goal? To find the center of the storm where calmness reigns, even though the winds swirl about? It is possible. You can travel in the eye of the storm and never get caught up in the commotion. Others step outside the center and are quickly knocked off their feet. The center is always there, calling you back: "Come here and find refuge. Be still and rest awhile."

The Great "I" always lies within. It is why you are so uncomfortable when all is in turmoil, for you are off center. You need not grasp and crawl and struggle to get back to the I. You need merely acknowledge that the I is your home and that you wish to rest there. In this awareness and by making this choice, instantly you are transported home.

*September 7*

## RESONANCE

Take away the bodies and you would still recognize each other. You have your individual energy signature that all in spirit can read like a book. Every detail is known by the vibration. Even now you experience a bit of this. Do you not feel a person's energy when you meet them? You are attracted to some and repelled by others, but not by their appearance, by how they feel to you.

If you were to lose your physical sight, far greater would be your sensing ability in this regard. This you can increase now whilst still in physical form, by merely paying closer attention to your intuition. That is the eyes of the soul.

What do you want others to sense when they encounter you? Honesty or deception? Love or fear? You can hide now from some, but not forever. Work now to raise your vibration and observe how your resonance with all does increase.

*September 8*

## THE MESSAGE OF THE WOLF

Why do wolves howl at the moon? Because they are restless. Inside, their soul knows peace. Outwardly, they feel trapped. In their anguish they bay at the light in the sky calling them home, yet they remain earthbound.

Yes, they are pack animals, and they find great solace in these bonds, but inside they long for freedom. Do not feel sorry for the wolf. He is at home anywhere he roams. He will howl, yes, as if in anguish, but inside his soul knows the truth. He is strong. He is trustworthy.

He is loyal, but given a chance, given wings, he would fly to the moon and back. Why would he return? For once there he would discover that home is where the heart is. Not at some distant, glowing rock, but there inside him, where the glow never goes out.

*September 9*

## ALWAYS THERE

Leaves rustle when you walk through them. You kick them with your shoes, unaware that these are the husks of living things now discarded. The true essence of the leaf is no longer there. The living force has gone out of them and is being recycled all around you.

You go to your cemeteries and cry at the grave of your loved ones. Your think they lie there. With no disrespect we tell you this is just the husk, now discarded, to return to earth and be recycled. The true essence of the one you loved lives on and is there beside you as you talk to their grave. Know this when you sorrow: Your loved ones accompany you as you depart the gravesite. Wherever you go, as you hold them in your heart and mind, they are with you, for the spirit never dies and is never discarded.

The body served a purpose. It is well and good to revere it, but place your reverence first and foremost on Life—on the Spirit which animates you and your loved ones forever. It is this Spirit you will recognize when you see your loved ones again.

## TRY IT ON

Hallowed be thy name, for thy name is Christ. In this case, we speak to you, and we speak not of a person, but of a concept and a truth. You are all created in the image of your heavenly Creator, given the gift of love and creative ability. This is the true meaning of a Christ ... one who realizes this truth and embodies this truth in thought and action. Jesus the Christ did do so, did he not, as have other Masters throughout the ages, for the Truth is available to all.

Do you wish to know the Truth? Be it. Live it. Express it. It is only through personal experience that you have a personal relationship with the true Self and recognize who you truly are. Do not shy away from names, terms, and concepts based on past beliefs and what others tell you. Put on the cloak and try it for yourself. How does it fit, this mantle of Truth?

*September 11*

## LEAD THE WAY

It is easy for you to become discouraged when you are bombarded with images of mayhem. You despair and think the world is coming to an end. Humans have been hurting humans for as long as you can remember. This is what happens when humans have free will.

You are the light. Does this phrase bring you peace? It will if you have had the tiniest exposure to that light inside of you. Now turn it up. Turn it up when you see your news. Shine it toward those who cannot see the light. Be the light for those who can see no way out. Be a beacon for those lost in the dark.

There will be darkness as long as there is free will, but one day, when man no longer has any lessons to learn, there will no longer be a need for free will. Then all light will be revealed.

Light is eternal, and you are that light. Shine on brightly through the darkness and lead the way.

*September 12*

## LOVE MORE

You look to us this day when you are looking for answers, and this day we tell you to look at yourselves. Evil does not come from spirit. Anything less than love is a by-product of free will. It is all one energy. It is consciousness, and the conscious use of free will leads to acts which make the front page of your newspapers.

Once again we ask you: How will you respond? Now that you have turned to us, we repeat our oft-shared advice: Love more. "Oh, how naïve!" you cry as you stare, fascinated, at your headlines. And we ask you, will fearing more help? Will anger help? As a human, these emotions come naturally.

Imagine if all children were raised with naught but love, acceptance, and understanding of each other. Imagine if a society believed that these qualities are all that mattered. Imagine if these were taught from the first day of this school of life to the last and practiced by all of its students. Why, then, school would be out, for all would have learned the lessons.

Love more.

*September 13*

## PEACE

"Will it be okay? Will it all turn out right?" you ask as you wring your hands. We ask you to sit and breathe. Now please step back and see your situation from a higher perspective—from the place of stillness.

Your world is ever changing. Whether or not things are "okay" is a matter of perspective. Only in the stillness, where nothing changes, do you find true peace. Do not spend so much time in the future. Spend more time in the silence of now. Do this and you will learn that all simply is a playing out of scenarios in which to learn to find peace. A bit paradoxical, but all part of the adventure.

Everything is cyclical. Will it be okay? Yes, and then no, and then yes, and then no, from your perspective, and in between there is always peace. Always.

## CLARITY

Clear out the system. Get rid of any chemicals not needed. Drugs, alcohol, excessive sugar ... all of these when ingested to the point that they dull the senses dull the awareness of spirit. This seems obvious, does it not, but how many turn to dulling the senses over turning to spirit?

Spirit is always there. Great peace, great joy, great love can be had when one reunites with the spirit side of the being, yet so often spirit is unreachable due to physical impediments. Think of one who suffers from dementia. Spirit is alive and well, of course, but the physical brain blocks awareness. Rest assured, when freed of the physical body, all will be well and clear again, but for now there is a disconnect.

Do you feel disconnected from spirit now? Investigate the cause. It may be physical. Do what you can to clarify things, but in the meantime, know that were it not for spirit you would not breathe.

You are well looked after and loved beyond words.

*September 15*

## DOUBLY

A double-take. You know this expression. It comes with a shake of the head which says, "Did I really hear that or see that? Did that really happen?" Why did this catch your attention so? Because it is out of the ordinary or extraordinarily synchronistic.

Double your chances of extraordinary events by sitting in the singular silence of unity consciousness. It is only by knowing your oneness with all that is through the experience of it that you create such perfection and flow in your life that miracles become the norm.

Through the experience of duality you return to oneness and recognize unity. Take every opportunity to sit in the silence, blending with the One Divine Mind, and partake doubly of the miracle that is your life here and now.

## YOUR HEALING SANCTUARY

Healing does take place in the presence of higher energy. Frequency adjustments do happen in which the higher energies bring harmony where there is dis-ease. In the presence of love and the absence of fear these higher vibrations are felt.

Know that you can sustain these positive effects, not just when in the presence of another who brings in higher vibrations. Sit in the silence and bring the light to yourself. Move your focus away from your pain, be it physical or emotional, and focus on the light. Move your awareness beyond the physical to the realm of no-time, no-space, and there find relief. Stay there a while.

When you return to full waking consciousness, a bit of order will have been restored in addition to the calming state you experienced whilst fully bathed in the light. This is your healing sanctuary. Sit in it often. Ask for your healing angels to surround you and to follow you throughout the day.

Blessings be upon you.

*September 17*

## STILL DEVELOPING

You call them "developing countries." Developing toward what? More disconnection from each other thanks to the use of technology? More focus on the acquisition of material abundance? Do you think these things bring greater happiness and peace? Yes, it is good in your world to have running water, sanitation, and shelter, but once these are satisfied, how developed must you become before you declare, "I have arrived?"

Take a look at some of your least "developed" tribes. There you will find a connection between its members at a level most reading our words have never known. There you will find caring for multiple generations and for the neighbor. There you will find long moments spent sitting in communion. There you will find broad smiles.

Now, we ask you ... which parts of your life will you choose to develop today?

## NEVER-ENDING SUPPLY

From whence cometh envy? From the false belief that you do not have enough. The desire for material things comes from a need to fill a void. The void is merely the lack of awareness that you are essentially love.

When you awaken fully to the presence of Love as you, you will have no need for anything else or anyone else. Of course you will want to share this love you have discovered with others, and for that reason you will want to enjoy the company of others, but no longer will you feel envy of another who appears to have more than you do—only happiness for those who have also discovered Who they are.

If another's alleged greatness comes not from a place of love, then you will only feel compassion and the desire that they, too, will find the peace and love that only comes from within.

Envy signifies a misunderstanding, for there truly is no lack, but a never-ending supply ... of love.

*September 19*

## PROPPED UP

Adversity … those times when you struggle to maintain equanimity, balance. You are thrown off balance by a challenge. The natural inclination is to return to standing tall instead of falling. It is the law of balance.

You make every effort to right yourself, but sometimes you need a little propping up. Do not be afraid to ask for help, be it in the form of friends and family in the physical world or helpers in the non-physical.

You may have trouble standing on two feet, but you do not stand alone. You are not a solitary tree in the forest, but the forest itself. Realizing this will make it easier to stand. The winds may buffet you about, but allow the others around you to be your buffer.

Ask for help and you will receive it.

## BY THE GRACE OF GOD

Survival ... getting through a situation alive. It is a silly word, for there is no death. What you mean when you laugh and say, "I survived it," is that you are still here ... a bit wounded, perhaps, but also a bit changed.

Yes, you will survive. You will survive the trials of life, and they do come aplenty. You may come out a bit wounded, but look at the cut on your finger. How does it heal? Do you do anything or does it heal itself? You may help the process with a bit of salve and a bandage, but the skin grows over the cut. The two sides bind together as if by magic.

It is by the grace of God that wounds are healed, as are you from your troubles. It is not miraculous. It is because you are loved. And if wounds do not heal and the body dies? What a surprise: the soul lives on! And it continues growing and healing ... by the grace of God, for all there is is Love.

*September 21*

## NO STRINGS ATTACHED

Abandonment. What does this mean?

In your concept it means that another has left you—that they no longer need or want you. The very reading of these words brings pain to your heart. All humans want to be needed, wanted, and loved.

We wish you to know that when one human leaves another, it is merely through the physical presence. Once joined in love, you are always connected. It is your human attachments which cause you pain. You cling tightly to others, often out of fear and not true love.

If you were to let go of your fears and attachments, you could look inside and there find all the love you need. Feeling secure in your Self as the Source of love, all human beings could walk away from you and you would still be content, knowing that there is truly no separation.

When you cease clinging, let go of attachment, and allow love to simply flow, then you are truly free.

*September 22*

## KINDERGARTEN LESSONS

Give yourself the gift of patience. You are much harder on yourself than on others. You are a work in progress—a true work of art. God is molding you bit by bit with loving care. You want to rush the job and reach perfection now.

Would you rush the artist? Would you tell the sculptor to put a little tuck there, tell the painter to dab a little paint there? Perhaps you would. Your life is, indeed, a collaborative effort, but who has the greater picture? Who is unencumbered by duality—by ups and downs, highs and lows, and all of the other human experiences? You bring much to the Artist's studio, but do you really want to hold all of the brushes?

Do you remember painting with your fingers ... dipping into the gooey mess of color and simply swirling about wherever the spirit moved you? Relax, my friend, and let Spirit move you today. Be loose. Be guided. Swirl about with joy, for you are being perfectly crafted, even if all is not yet perfect in your eyes.

*September 23*

## FROM THE SHADOWS

You can run, but you cannot hide from your deepest fears, your anger, your demons. There is no real devil. There are only the lower, slower vibrations which exist as possibility, as does all Source energy.

It is your own consciousness which raises and lowers the vibrations. Some of the lower ones have been held for safe-keeping for a very long time in a place you would know as your sub-conscious. They rise to the level of awareness often at the most opportune time, which to you would seem to be the most inopportune.

"Hello," they announce, "I am here. Now what are you going to do with me?" Yes, what indeed? Know that you can always ask for help. That is why you are given life-long unseen helpers, but they will also stay in the shadows until invited in.

As for those devilish appearances, will you push them back into the shadows or deal with them now that they have made their presence known? Take control of what comes out of the shadows and it can control you no more.

## PATTERNS

Do not be afraid to move on.

Yes, you may have made mistakes in what you know as the past, but the past does not exist, save in your consciousness. Let it go. It holds no power unless you hold onto it. Then it becomes a pattern, for you continue to play it over and over in the mind, bringing it into your present now as if it is real.

What is real? You create reality in your mind. Is what you call the past a reality you wish to repeat or not? If so, continue acting and thinking as you do. If not, see the past as obsolete and create this moment anew.

Flood your consciousness with fresh, bright light and pull it through you, cleansing the body of unwanted energy. From this bright, clear space, step out boldly and create new patterns.

*September 25*

## ALLOWING

There is not just you in this world. And yet, you think that all others think as you do. When they say and do things that would not have been what you would say and do, you are shocked, affronted, disappointed. "How could they do such a thing?!"

They could do such a thing for they have free will. They are here to express Consciousness, as are you. You call it "playing God" when one tries to control others and events. You are not in human form to play God ... you are in human form for God to play as you. There is quite a difference.

You play as God in form, but you are not the entirety of God. All of you make up aspects of the Great Spirit, and as such there are billions of modes of expression. How others choose to express their Godliness is up to them. That is the beauty of it all.

Allow, allow, allow them to do so. When others make choices and decisions contrary to those you would have made, allow these expressions of Consciousness, knowing that all is in Divine order. Sit back, breathe deeply, and observe the expressions of Life in peace.

## GROWING GRACEFULLY

The leaves of autumn blow about, so dry and brittle are they. They will return to dust, only to be replaced in the Spring by new shoots. All of life is like this. The human body comes in green and lithe and over time becomes brittle. This cannot be stopped, and why would you want it to? Ah, yes, because you think that falling from the tree is the end of the story. Yes, for the leaf's structure it is the end, but the energetic pattern of the leaf remains. You merely cannot see it.

What reappears in the springtime is following a pattern of consciousness. Do you not see how all of life is like this, including your own? You fear your demise, but it is only the demise of the body, not your pattern and most certainly not your consciousness. You as spirit cannot grow brittle and die. You are, indeed, forever young in spirit.

You grow eternally, yet never age in physical terms as you know it. May you find comfort in this knowledge. Allow the body to age gracefully as you accept the grace of God in giving you eternal life.

*September 27*

## GREATER AND GREATER

Joy such as you have never known awaits you. This is the point of life. Are you not ever learning? What do you learn? Greater and greater knowledge, wisdom, strength, coping skills, and so on. The point is: learning is about "greater and greater" ... constant upward growth.

All of life is about learning to express your true nature, which is Love. Joy is experienced in this expression. You may slip back a bit now and then in your learning, but always the thrust is upward and onward. And so, greater and greater joy awaits you.

But wait! Are you not now wiser than in the past? Have you not grown? Do you not have the capacity to love even more now than in the past? Of course you do. So enjoy this moment fully. Sit in the joy, but know that greater and greater joy is guaranteed.

Yes, of course there will be great challenges along the way. You are facing some now, but amidst the pain there will always be a glimpse of the joy that is ever-present and ever awaiting.

That is Life. Enjoy It.

## IN AND OUT

In and out, in and out. The body is a perfect instrument for taking in what it needs and excreting what it does not. You do this with the breath, with your water, with your food. Even when you cry, you excrete toxins through the nose and eyes, refreshing the body.

Do not diminish the importance of clearing the bodies -- mental, emotional, spiritual, and physical. All moves in a cyclical fashion, coming and going. When energy gets jammed up and dammed up inside of the body, disharmony results. Keep it moving. Move the physical body in exercise, bringing in fresh air. Flush the body with pure water, replenish it with health-giving foods, and feast upon joyful thoughts. This is the prescription for wellness.

In and out. Breathe in the goodness of life and exhale that which no longer serves you.

*September 29*

## EVER-PRESENT

Do not allow your fears to consume you. This is quite easy to do when you forget you are spirit in human form. In the forgetting, ego takes over, and ego loves fear. It holds you prisoner.

When you are tied up in your fears it is difficult to feel your true nature and to express it. Love is held at bay whilst you fret about what is yet to come. Perhaps the things you fear may come to pass and perhaps they will not.

What is happening now? Are you fully present now? Can you take a deep breath and be fear-free for a few moments? Now carry that feeling with you to the next moment. Was that so bad? The future arrived and here you are again, now. And how do you deal with now, now? In the same manner.

Take a breath. Be present, and remember who you are. All else will come and go, but you as the love of God are ever-present.

## TURNING PAGES

And in the end, there is only one thing that matters ... did you grow? That is why you are here. Happily, growth comes naturally, so there is all likelihood that you will succeed in this chapter of your life.

Note that we call it a chapter, for there is no final chapter and no real end, merely a turning of the page for a new beginning ... a cliff-hanger, we hope as you eagerly anticipate more to follow, with greater growth in the ongoing story of you.

Learn all that you can while you are here. Soak up the lessons. Grow greatly in your capacity to love yourself and others, and yours will be the greatest story ever told.

## STRING THEORY

Never fear, for help is here
Closer than you think.
It's at your side, inside your heart
As fast as you can blink.

You cannot get away from it
This help that's at your call
For you're supremely linked, my friend,
With what's the Source of all.

See the strands made up of light.
See them linked as one—
One big web of which you're part
That cannot be undone.

Your cries for help don't go unheard
They travel down the strands
Reverberating outward
Like vibrating rubber bands.

This vibration carries messages
To exactly where they're needed
And back across the strands come help
For by your thoughts this help 'twas seeded.

## LET IT BE

Do you have regrets? Most likely the answer is yes, for all of you are human. How do you deal with a perceived mistake? Let it be. Let it be. Ah yes, another of your songs with great wisdom.

Can you allow your past actions to simply be instead of giving them a life of their own and taking up residence with them? Can you do the same with the actions of others? There is far greater peace when you can simply be.

Be in the moment now, and if you should slip into the past and find a regret or two or three, let it be, let it be.

*October 3*

## RULES

Relax the rules. Most of you are quite unaware of how many rules you impose on this Game of Life. When others fail to follow the rules which you see as sacrosanct, you become upset. The jaw clenches. In so being, you have restricted the unfoldment of greater possibilities.

"But," you protest, "without rules, there would be chaos!" In some cases, perhaps, but today we ask you to make a list of just a few of the rules you impose on yourself and others. Now study them and see if you might paint outside the box just a bit. Can you do so without experiencing fear? The fear is a sign that you are clinging to a rule. How interesting.

Make a game of this activity: "Find the Hidden Rules." Then open up to possibilities. Enjoy the freedom of allowing, for from your viewpoint greater possibilities are often obscured. Allow Higher Consciousness to guide the outcome. Without so many rules, you may just be delightfully pleased at the results.

## GETTING TO THE ESSENCE

You fear that there is not enough love in your world. Fear not! Love is the essence of your world. Get out in nature and look around you. What is the Source of such beauty?

With love in your heart, look at your children, your brothers, your sisters, your elders. Again, what is the Source of such beauty? Love is the essence of all creation. It becomes hidden as the human exerts free will and makes choices not in resonance with the higher vibrations. Do not allow yourself to become dragged down by these baser vibrations.

Where you place your focus becomes your reality. Is it a world of love or otherwise? Perception is reality. Choose to see the love and be the love in your world, and that is the world you will experience.

*October 5*

## GETTING CENTERED

When your world tumbles about you and all is filled with discord, seek balance. Where do you find balance in any shape? At the center. Go there, my friend, and rest a while. It is quite easy to find yourself at the outer edges, propelled there by momentum. It takes a deliberate effort to stop the inertia and retreat back to the center.

From the calm eye of the storm you can ask for guidance and get back on a more favorable course. Go there often to this place of peace when all swirls about you, and you will not lose your balance.

It is never too late to get centered.

## LIGHTING UP THE GRID

There are no accidents.

Each one whose path you cross was put there for a reason. Look how very interconnected you are. There are infinite links in this web of circuits of which you are a part. Reaching out, you help to light up circuit after circuit until it becomes a teeming grid of light so bright that it can be felt around the world.

How will you do your part to light up the grid? A simple loving thought is a good place to start, and the next thing you know, that thought sets fire, spreading its flames and bringing in yet more Light.

Shine on ever more brightly, but be not surprised as the effects of your Light bring greater and greater synchronicities, greater connections. That is how Life works when you employ the greatest fire-starter of all: Love.

## October 7

### YOUR GREATEST RESPONSIBILITY

Responsibility goes in all directions. If you truly wish to change things, you have a responsibility to your children, to your parents, to your friends, your family, and to yourself. Why is this? All is one. What affects one affects all of you.

You all understand fear, and grief, and anger, and love, for you all have felt these. How can billions of people feel and understand the very same emotions? For the separation between you is an illusion. Yes, you all feel or do not feel emotions in varying degrees based upon the level you have let ego take precedence over the spirit, but all of you came into this life as the essence of love.

Due to free will and the influence of those around you, your understanding and expression of love has diverged from that purity. Getting back to that pure essence is your major task in life. Helping others to find it within themselves will help you as well. Why? Because there is no separation. It is all the self-same Force which animates all of you or you would not cry out so loudly when love is absent.

Keep seeking this Force, and in so doing you will learn to express it. In so doing, you will learn that you ARE it.

## OUT OF IGNORANCE

A weapon is nothing but an inert mass until the holder of that weapon makes a choice to use it. This is free will. Once that choice is made to harm another, any weapon will do.

Life is sacred. Why is this so, if life is eternal? All life is an expression of God, and God is, indeed, Love. You are part of That. Your brother and sister are part of That. The little ant that walks on your finger unaware that you exist is part of That. You go on and on into eternity, existing for the very purpose that God is Love and wishes to experience its true nature through you.

To use free will to express anything less than your true nature shows ignorance of who you are and why you are here. This ignorance is not to be condemned, but seen with compassion. If the ignorant were able to feel compassion, they would not be ignorant, nor would they be capable of harming another.

Your task is to help all to open their eyes and see the sacredness of life. Killing does not end life, but it does end the opportunity to grow in loving and to express love here and now. In your grief, may there be awakening to the reason you are all here, and may more love be felt as a result. In this way, may good come of expressions of ignorance.

*October 9*

## IN THE STILLNESS

"Be still, and know that I am God." This phrase you have heard before. And have we not shared with you the phrase, "I am That"? And now, hearing this, some of you will want to run out and do what you call "playing God." You will want to control all situations, for you reason, "I am That!"

In fact, being a part of That calls for just the opposite. This is the part referred to as "being still." Be still and allow the greater aspect of the self—the part that has no need to control—to be in control. Hmmm. Yet another paradox.

Ego wants to control. Spirit unfolds in the stillness as all parts of the All work together, not just one individual aspect. Surrender to the knowledge that you are a part of That, and allow yourself to be guided … gently at times and unmistakably at others, but always from the stillness … that place of peace, not angst, that speaks to you softly and says, "All is well."

## THE ORDERLY STAGE

When you knock upon a door, it is opened. Alas, it is not always opened by the one you expect. You are not alone in this adventure you call life. Others play vital roles. All are cells in the body of the Creator, all serving the greater good.

At times you only see your influence upon what is most near and dear to you. As a part of the whole, your influence and role is far greater than you imagine. It is not diminished because there are so many others, but increased in value for the greatness you make up as a whole.

Realize that your desires may at times conflict with those of others. Know that all is in perfect order and that order will always reign. There is a Director of this great play who loves all of the actors. If you stumble and bump into the role of another upon the stage from time to time, consult the Director. All will be sorted out in favor of the grand production. It is the Law … the Law of Love.

*October 11*

## SACRED SOUND

Chanting. We ask you to give it a try. Why? For in the act of repeating a sound, you experience the act of creation. You come to a greater understanding of the Creator and of yourself as the same.

Find a quiet place. Relax the body. Breathe deeply for a few moments, then choose the sound of creation to begin: Om. A perfect vibration. Your body will be well pleased with how this feels as you string one tone after another. And then, as you intone this sacred sound, you will begin to understand how life works. From the silence arises a vibration. After it has been created, it is sustained. Consciousness determines the length of its existence. And then, after the fullness of experience, it returns to the silence, the cycle complete. Like all cycles, it begins again: creation, sustainment, and extinction. Om. Om. Om.

You may create a burst of short chants, or sustain many long tones in a row. Do you see how you create? Always from the silence, and always back to the silence does the vibration return, again and again. And what is doing the creating? Consciousness. What is that which is created? The Word.

Play with Om and experience God.

## ONE SOURCE

When you look upon another,
There I AM.
When you gaze into the eyes of a lover,
There I AM.

When you stroke another's face,
There I AM.
When you behold the human race,
There I AM.

There is nowhere you can gaze That I AM not.
This is the only lesson you've forgot.
When you can take these words and know them in your heart.
Then you will know that You and I can never be apart.

Take these words and hold them to your chest.
With this knowing in your heart you now can rest.
For all is One and nothing ever dies.
From the one Source all love and life it does arise.

*October 13*

## MONKEY BUSINESS

Monkeys swing from branch to branch, oft jumping as if flying through the spaces in between. Such freedom they do enjoy. Their life seems like all play and games. They sit up high and view the world with curiosity. Could you not learn a lesson from these creatures?

Invite a bit of playfulness into your life. Monkey around a bit. Why are you so serious all the time? Be free to jump from branch to branch, exploring new ways of being, new ways of seeing from new vantage points.

Rest a while in these new ways of being. Sit and scratch your head. It is quite curious, this new vantage point, is it not? Now screech. Let the world hear your voice, and do not forget to laugh. There is a lot to be learned from God's creatures, is there not?

## ALWAYS IN CONTROL

At times your life goes off in directions you did not foresee. At times you feel a bit out of control. Never forget that it is not you who controls this great drama you call life. You play a vital part, but the drama would not exist, save for the Director.

When things pick up speed and begin to careen, take your foot off the pedal and coast. In these moments of easing off, remember who is truly doing the driving. In that knowledge, relax, take deep breaths, and then surrender the need to feel frenzied.

There is no need to do anything other than take one step at a time, knowing you are always guided. There is no need to control anything. Loosen the reins and give your full faith and trust to the One which reigns over all.

*October 15*

## THE MAGIC OF CREATION

Mickey Mouse is one of your cartoon figures, created by a man of great vision—a man who had an idea and allowed it to grow into an empire. This Walt Disney created a kingdom, did he not? A magic kingdom where happiness reigns, filled with laughter, and joy, and colorful characters that make children smile. All of this from one little mouse.

"That is a Mickey Mouse concept," you sometimes hear, and in this case, the term is a bit derogatory, meaning small and somewhat silly. Do you see how ideas take on their own lives? They begin as seeds of consciousness and grow, depending upon how they are nurtured along the way by all of the interconnected minds that handle this seed of an idea.

Do you not see now how the kingdom truly does lie within? Will you birth Mickey Mouse ideas as silly and inconsequential, or as grand creations which go on to produce joy, laughter, and love in your world?

It truly is a magic kingdom when you use the magic wand within your limitless mind and create miracles.

## LIKE A CHILD

A baby's smile lights up a room. So innocent are they. They draw those around them like a magnet. You want to touch their tiny toes, to stroke their hair, and to cuddle them to the breast. Why this attraction? It is the innocence. The purity.

These new-born souls are the mirror of your soul. You look at them and there is a recognition, and yes, desire. "Wouldn't it be nice to have no worries? To be so innocent?"

You can return to this state of grace at any time simply by shifting your consciousness from earthly concerns to the realm of Spirit. It is in you now. Access it with a simple shift in focus. Aha. There is the tiny child—that seed of innocence and pure love. That pearl is who you are. Tiny babies are mere reminders.

Set your worries aside for a moment and be childlike. This short respite is indeed rejuvenating on multiple levels. Be young at heart, for your soul is ageless.

*October 17*

## SURF ON

What makes a wave rise? It is your laws of physics. Laws are in effect in all aspects of your world. Were this not so, there would not be growth, only chaos. Due to the laws of nature and the Law of Love, there is growth ever upward. You call this "evolution."

At the present time you are experiencing a surge in the evolution of human consciousness. Jump on your surfboard, my friend, and ride this wave. Stand fearlessly at the crest and call to those below you: "Come along! It is not as frightening as it seems! In fact, it is quite exhilarating."

As you push aside the fear of new experiences and new beliefs, you help to raise your consciousness and that of those around you. Ride the wave, for it will take you to new heights of love, to new heights of understanding. Once you have achieved each new level of mastery, there is no turning back. Then you will realize that the ride is endless and ever enjoyable.

Surf on.

IN DIGESTION . . .

A Happy Meal – a special meal you purchase for your children to make them smile. It contains a toy—a tiny treasure to bring joy.

Why are your adult meals often so joyless? You eat without mindfulness. Do you pay attention as your nourishment enters the body? Do you feel gratitude for the source of your food and the miracle of digestion? Do you share high vibrations with those who share your meal or is there disharmony? This, of course, affects the digestion.

In all of your actions, practice mindfulness. Be aware of the miracle of life, instead of driving on auto-pilot. Savor every bit of this earthly experience, whether it be a happy meal or a challenging learning experience. Digest your adventures fully, and grow all the more strong as a result.

*October 19*

## BECAUSE YOU LOVE

One of your greatest challenges is to sit back and observe whilst one you love suffers through their own challenges. Why do you wish to help? Because you have suffered yourself and you wish to save them from pain. You have learned. You have gained wisdom and can see a better way for them.

Yes, you can help. Feel free to do so. Offer loving advice as it feels right in your heart to do so, but when met with resistance or when the other does not "hear" you, see this as a message from the soul of the one you love that the human being attached to that soul is working through their lessons still. The resistance is not a personal affront, although in many cases it will come across in that way. Do your best to not internalize the other's pain. Send only love—that greatest of healing energy. The soul will receive it, if not the human ego.

Can you practice detached compassion and allow your loved one to grow as you send love? If not, you will experience your own pain and stunted growth. Do you see how you grow together ... how very interconnected you are? Grow in love. It is love which binds you, or you would not feel the pain. But know that pain need not be ever-present. Practice the art of allowing life and its lessons to unfold, loving ever more deeply as you do so.

## TRADITIONS OLD AND NEW

Traditions … carried down from one generation to the next. Why do they last? For they bring connection, learning, a sense of belonging. You mourn when traditions die away, and with good reason. When there is no tradition, there is separation. Think of your Thanksgiving traditions … togetherness.

If traditions no longer serve you, then make new ones. How can you find unity? How can you connect with the heart, the soul of others? All things have their time. They fade. But love, connection, relationship is not a thing—it is a state of being. Savor it, and save it through traditions, old or new.

*October 21*

## THE COST OF ADMISSION

Freedom comes with a price. Surrender of the ego is the admission fee to Heaven. Heaven is where you are when you finally discover that Love is all that matters.

When you can put this realization into practice and see and feel and be Love in every moment, with no need to interject the limited ego self into the picture, then you are free. Then you can fly, for then you have earned your wings.

The ego is necessary to operate in the physical world. It is not your enemy, but it is far from the greatest part of you. You are Spirit. You are Love. You are everywhere. The ego does not connect with others. The ego erects barriers.

Spirit is pure Love. It knows no boundaries, has no barriers. It is free. Ego pays the price of separation and pain. Surrender ego in every moment that you experience pain, and turn up the love, no matter how difficult.

Heaven awaits. Enter now. The cost of admission is well worth it.

## LETTING GO

Why are you so often disappointed? Because you have expectations.

From whence come these desires? From the ego. Ego says, "I want this to happen a certain way. I want this person to do a certain thing." Always it is your way and your desire for your outcome. Of course, when this does not come about, you experience dissatisfaction and disappointment.

How often do you simply surrender and allow others to be themselves? They are here for their own experiences and growth. God revels in diversity. It is the ego which rebels.

Relax a bit. Can you do this? Your Creator does not worry or experience frustration. When you experience these lesser vibrations, recognize the ego in action. To find satisfaction and peace, learn to allow all outside of yourself to unfold as it will.

With release comes peace.

*October 23*

RIDE IT OUT

After the storm comes the calm. This is a law of nature ... something upon which you can rely when the winds swirl about you. You know that you need only bide your time, and peace will once again prevail.

The same is true of this situation in which you find yourself. All of life is changing. Were nothing to ever change, there would be no growth. Know that this too shall pass. The outcome may not be as you would wish, but peace will eventually come. All will be resolved, to give rise to a new adventure.

Things may seem hopeless when you are in the thick of the storm, but the clouds do eventually part. Do not lose hope. The sun is always inside, awaiting your recognition. When you recognize this, the storm passes even sooner.

## CONFLICT RESOLUTION

Conflict arises when two or more do not see eye to eye. You have different ways of approaching the same goal. One wishes to go in one direction, the other in another. Oft times there is confusion about the destination itself. The more you diverge, the more negativity surrounds the situation, and like magnets repelling each other, you cannot seem to come together. This is called reverse polarity. It does not work.

So what is the solution? Agree to disagree. Meet in the middle and set new goals, even if this means a parting of the ways. Surround the situation with love and surround the one with whom you feel in conflict with well wishes.

You do not all walk the same path. You will eventually discover the reason your paths did cross, but cross they did—at an angle, not in parallel. This you call conflict, but there is a reason for every meeting, every crossing. What have you learned? See the situation not with bitterness, but as yet another learning point in this school you call Life.

*October 25*

## STEP IN AND REACH OUT

Never be afraid to enlist the help of friends or strangers. Yes, of course use caution with strangers, but let your heart be your guide. Our point is that in reaching out, you lessen your fear and strengthen your connection with All That Is.

Whoever you reach out to is part of the same Source from which you come. Why would you not wish to tap into the greater aspect of you? Why do you stand back? Who taught you this unusual behavior?

Overcome your hesitation—this learned belief that you are not part of one big and beautiful Whole—and step into the circle of Love.

SPARKLES

And so, you judge.

You look upon another and form an opinion. Usually that opinion is based upon the variance between others' actions, appearance, or words in relation to your own. When you judge, your actions, appearance, and words become the standard.

When we tell you that you are a manifestation of God, we do not mean that you are the entirety of God. How could that be, when God is All That Is? In making yourself the reference, you are singling out one aspect of God without remembering that all that you see is also a reference point.

You are all facets of the same Jewel. Does one facet of a diamond judge another? In your world, perhaps, but know that the Diamond does not judge Itself or Its individual parts. It merely sparkles. Sit back, judge not, and simply sparkle.

*October 27*

RISE

"Why do some face more challenges than others?" you ask. It is because they can handle it, and more will be the growth of those around them for it. These special souls did enter this life agreeing to take on more than their share, for they realized what lessons in love these challenges would be.

It is the nature of the human being to forget these agreements when you dress in a body, but the spirit knows that all challenges are opportunities for the growth of many, not just the one. When you pass from the body, you will all see how intricately all fits together and what an important role your challenges played in the growth of many souls.

How one handles challenges depends greatly on one's perception. It is always a choice to view a challenge as a tragedy or an opportunity. Step back from your human reaction and see with the eyes of Spirit. Rather than sinking into the depths of despair, flood all situations with love, then rise to the surface and breathe.

## THE BOTTOM LINE

It all comes down to love. That is the bottom line, and the top, and the middle.

Why are the majority of your song lyrics focused on this subject? Why do all struggle at some point in their lives to find it? Why is it the motivating force behind all efforts, whether recognized or not? It is because love is an actual energy, a force, a thing. It forms life, itself. It is Life, itself.

All comes into being because of or out of love, and you are that. When you react out of love, you are at your most peaceful and genuine, for you are no longer living a lie that denies your true Self. Be loving. Be love, itself. Be yourself, and you cannot go wrong.

Love cannot be harmed. Love cannot die. Love simply is. It is a state of being. It is being, itself. Now go back and reread these words. In doing so, substitute any word you have every used for "God" in place of the word "love," and perhaps you will understand why it is said that God is Love.

*October 29*

## LEARNING TO SAY NO

It feels good to say yes to others. They respond with a smile. You fill their needs and thus feel needed. But what of your needs? When you continuously fill the needs of others and deny the self, you deplete the self.

Energy flows in both directions. Be aware of when it is out of balance. Realize that you need not always say yes. Others will still love you. You are far more able to give of the self—to give love—when you are in balance.

No is not always a negative word. There are gentle ways of saying no— of saying no with love. In doing so, you are enabling the self to recharge. You are saying, "I know that I am loved no matter what I say to this other. They are responsible for their own growth. I can say yes or no to their needs, yet still send them my love, and thus be of service."

What is it your flight attendants tell you to do in the case of the deployment of your oxygen mask? If there is one in need seated beside you, you cannot help them unless you help yourself first.

Seek balance so that you remain always filled with love.

## TUNE IN

Music soothes the savage beast. So why do you listen to savage music? Choose the tones you listen to wisely. They do affect your consciousness. The vibrations of each note can be harmful or healing, depending on the way in which they are arranged.

How does the song make you feel? Energized or enervated? Peaceful and calm or crazed? You are not a slave to the radio. Turn it off or tune it to a tune that helps rejuvenate and energize you.

Choose tunes for meditation that help to bring your energy into balance. How will you know if the tunes are doing so? How do you feel when you listen to them? Get into the habit of listening to your body. It plays a non-stop tune with its vibration. Tune into that with awareness and you become the conductor of life instead of merely sitting in the bandstand.

*October 31*

## EXPOSURE

Every day you walk about in a body is a Halloween. Which mask will you wear today? You are given this costume to learn. You can use it any way you wish, for along with the body-costume comes free will. Will you use it to hide behind or to shine behind? Will you allow your true nature to peek through the two holes at the top of the face mask, or will you put a false smile upon the lips?

It is uncomfortable to wear a costume for too long. As the true self grows, you can no longer stand to wear the mask. Some day you get to the point where you must remove it completely and expose your self. As long as that is a frightening thought, you are not quite ready, and that is all right. Peel it back bit by bit or rip it off … at your own speed.

Working toward that goal is why you are here. Be patient with yourself as you peek out from behind the costume. Recognizing the costume for what it is is a step in the right direction.

## AUTOMATIC REACTIONS

You run from the skunk. History has told you that he is an enemy. You see the shape and the coloring and you bristle in horror. Even though you may never have encountered one face to face, you feel fear. Do you not know that the skunk's emission of an odor is a protective measure? He will walk by you placidly and perhaps even nuzzle your hand if met with love. It is your reaction and the fearful vibrations you emit that cause the skunk to emit the smell.

Can you not see how your interactions with your fellow man are the same? Have you not heard of so-called dangerous felons reacting not dangerously when met with love ... with them turning the cheek and walking the other way? We are not recommending that you walk into a skunk's den. We merely wish you to go on the offensive ... with love!

Do not be so quick to react to another's external stripes, lest he lash out protectively in response to your own fear. Radiate love at all times and the air around you will be all the more sweet.

*November 2*

## DETACHED, BUT WITH COMPASSION

When you watch your dramas on television or in your theaters, how do you feel at the end? If it was a comedy, are you not uplifted? If it was a horror show, are you not horrified? And if it had a sad ending, do you not desire to cry? Why, it was not even your story, and yet you react as if it was.

This is how empathy works. You take on the thoughts and feelings of other people's dramas. This is not always good for the soul. Can you be compassionate as you help others with their circumstances without getting caught up in the ups and downs of their drama? Yes, it is possible and most highly recommended. It is called practicing detached compassion.

You can send all of the love that is you without taking yourself on a roller coaster ride. Such rides are found at amusement parks, and they are amusing, yes. But after a while the ups and downs can and oft do make the body sick.

Be aware of being caught in others' drama and be compassionately detached.

## HEAT

Moses came upon a burning bush. The flames burned and burned, yet the bush was not consumed. You may interpret your Bible stories literally or figuratively. We wish you to know that the same Flame burns within you and speaks to you at all times.

Why does the body feel warm when enlivened with Spirit and cold to the touch when no longer animated by the Light? Your medical doctors would have a scientific explanation for this phenomenon, and yes, it is true: the molecules of the physical body vibrate and cause warmth, but we ask you: what causes those molecules to vibrate in the first place? The First Cause breathes Life into you and keeps your light burning.

Know that when the body turns cold, the Light continues in another reality where the physical sensations of hot and cold do not exist. It continues as a flame that cannot be extinguished—the eternal flame of your existence.

Place your hand on your heart and feel the heat, knowing that when you take the hand away, spirit remains, ever burning. Fan the flames with love and you will know this truth.

*November 4*

## CLOGGED UP

Syrup and molasses—slow moving, viscous liquids which you know as "sticky." Your energy is like this at times. It is then that you feel lethargic, out of sorts, and disconnected from others and your Source. The source of this sluggishness is varied, but remember that all is energy, including your thoughts.

Either your thoughts or the vibrations of others contribute to the stickiness of your vital force. How to unclog it? Chakra clearing is good. The mental shower of energy is good. Prolonged meditation combining the two is good. A walk in nature combined with deep breathing is good.

Key to all is conscious awareness that your vital energy is not flowing as clearly as it could be. An outside energy healer may be helpful. Do remember that there will be highs and lows, for even energy flows like a pendulum. Do what you can to keep the flow going well, knowing that your conscious efforts to do so will help the pendulum to swing in your favor more rapidly.

## THE ETERNAL FLAME

Lift up your eyes. What do you see? A light or darkness? Even in the darkest of places there is a glimmer. You call this hope. We call this home. Follow the tug that pulls you toward that glow and there you will find peace, even in the midst of chaos.

It is your pilot light, always there waiting to be turned up. In a moment it can go from a glimmer to a glow to a full-force flame. You ignite it with the recognition that it is there ...with the recognition that it burns inside of you ... with the recognition that you are never alone, and hence the warmth.

Allow the Pilot Light to guide you, to carry you to that place of peace, and know no fear, no worry, no discouragement. This is the one true Eternal Flame. May its warmth be felt today and every day as you travel this journey not alone, but safely protected in the arms of love.

*November 6*

## SELF-GENERATING

All is vibration. The leaf trembles. This is vibration. A bird sings and warbles. This is vibration. A street light flickers. This is vibration. Your heart beats. This is vibration.

What causes the fluttering, the quivering, the beating? The Great Energy Generator. It is a kinetic energy—energy without end—the bottomless Source. The heart may stop beating, but you go on vibrating, pulsating, quivering, for you are Life itself, that Force that cannot be extinguished.

Your scientists have not yet detected the Source of this energy. Like your gravity, they cannot explain it; you merely know that it exists. So use it, this Life Force. Call it what you want. We choose to call it Love.

May your heart today quiver with the Force of your love. If you could feel the full Force of the Love that keeps your heart beating, you would fall to your knees. Instead, stand tall and be your own generator of this love-energy.

## GOOD HABITS

You brush your teeth every day. This avoids a bad taste and a sticky feeling. Not all of you floss, for the results are not immediate. If it weren't for the bad taste and breath, not all of you would even brush. We apologize for the very mundane analogy, but do you see our point? Often the human needs a negative to propel you to do something positive. You may know that an action is good for you, but fail to take it if the reward is not instantaneous.

Know that every time you send love to one who does not love you in return or immediately give you a loving response, you are helping yourself and that other. It is like flossing the teeth. You have removed that which is damaging, in the way of lesser vibrations. You are helping the soul to shine.

It is a good habit to get into every day—this sending out your love instead of holding it inside for only the most worthy. Shine on as brightly as possible. You will find that once you have developed the habit, the rewards are, in fact, nearly instantaneous and far more far-reaching than you realize.

*November 8*

## NEW SHOES

Embarking on a trip is never easy. Exciting at times, yes, but not without a bit of trepidation. Fear not. It is the unknown that brings fright. You grow far too comfortable in your house slippers. Peel them off and step out in new shoes. They may take a bit of breaking in, but they will wrap around your feet just right after a while. And what happens then?

After a while you will have grown—and grown used to these new shoes as well. Time to trade them in for a sturdier pair of boots and march on with confidence. Life is like that—always asking you to readjust, to set aside that with which you have become comfortable, and strike out in new directions.

Enjoy a little comfort for a while, then challenge yourself. Challenge is good for the soul. Ego likes its soft slippers. There is nothing wrong with a little comfort, but you are here to stretch and grow. Beware of growing too comfortable.

## SHOULDS

Your expectations cause you angst. You think you know exactly how something should turn out. You place upon a situation and upon other people all of your "shoulds." And do not others place their "shoulds" upon you as well? What if these "shoulds" should conflict? Then you will surely encounter conflict.

"Too many chiefs and not enough Indians." One of your humorous phrases, but very wise when you are experiencing conflict. Do you wish to deconflict your life? Set aside your expectations and all of the "shoulds" – even those you place upon yourself.

Now relax and let the one Chief guide you. "Thy will be done, oh Wise One," would be an excellent attitude to start with. Then sit back and unwind. Delegation is a wonderful thing, and your Source never minds carrying your burdens for you.

*November 10*

## HOW'S THE WEATHER?

Mastery of the emotions is a lofty goal. To hold a steady state of peace is nigh unto impossible for the average human. Strive for perfection, if you please, but be quite pleased to merely be aware of your emotions from moment to moment.

Pay attention to your body. This is your barometer. Is the pressure high or low? Are you comfortable or not? You adjust the settings. Those around you and events around you can set off alarms. It is up to you to sense the alarms and adjust your reactions.

Do you enjoy drama? Then, by all means, keep your settings on high. But beware of the effect of high emotions on the physical body. Do you wish instead for more peace? Pay attention to your human weather station.

## EXPECTING THE BEST

"There is only one person who can help me," you think, and when that person is not available or does not give you the answer you expected, you are disappointed. You feel yet more despair. This is because you had expectations in the first place.

Do not feel bad about expecting to feel better, only be aware that it is your expectations about HOW to feel better that may lead to the disappointment. You do not always see the big picture. Your expectations oft come from a smaller perspective.

Disappointment is a sign—a sign that you are not attuned to your Higher Self. That aching feeling is a wake-up call. To move beyond the lower vibration of disappointment, recognize that you do not always know best when you come from a place of ego—the smaller self.

Set aside ALL expectations and surrender the ego to your Higher Self. That is the place of all possibility. It is also the place of all wisdom and all answers. The smaller "you" may not know what is best, and thus sets up limiting expectations. The greater You has the answers you seek.

Release all expectations of outcome. Surrender and allow the Best to unfold. You will not be disappointed.

*November 12*

## ROUND AND ROUND

Oneness is not a word, but a state of being—an experience of utter connectedness.

Is the circle not the perfect symbol? Where does the circle begin and end? Yes, you can take a pen and place the point on individual points along the surface of the circle or sphere and say, "Look at this dot—it is separate." But step back and see that the spot is an integral part, as are all other dots and spots on the sphere—all part of the one. Is any part greater or lesser? All make up the Whole—the One.

You are a dot, a spot, a point in time for a while as you experience mortal existence, but eternally part of the One which is your Source. Look upon all others and see them as no different from you when you take away the physical and mental characteristics that seem to separate you. Why bother? Because it is a circle of ever-flowing Love. When you do not understand this, you cut yourself off from the flow.

Each of you arises from the same well, the same Source. Seeing yourself as separate cuts off the Supply in your mind. You need merely open your mind to the Truth of your Oneness to flourish.

## THE ONE TRUE CAUSE

What is evil, but the lack of recognition of God. Evil does not exist as a thing. It is an effect—an outcropping. What you judge as evil was caused by ignorance.

You need not condone ignorance and its effect, but you can understand it. See it in the greater picture as the outcropping of the mass consciousness of humanity accepting the false belief in your separateness.

Evil is the outward expression of pain. Pain disappears when one understands that Love is the true Essence of all. Until that awakening occurs, pain is experienced. The effect is what you know as evil and the low vibrations of anger, judgment, and fear. Even the acknowledgment of these effects lowers your vibration. You can feel this, can you not?

Therefore, give no power to effects of falsehoods. Give power only to Love, for Love is all that is truly real—the only real Cause. Give all power to Love, and reap the effects of eternal peace.

*November 14*

FREE REIN

Cowboys on their horses gallop about the plains with such freedom. Look at the cooperation between man and beast. The horse has something to offer man, and they work together. Man cares for the horse in return.

All of life is about interrelationships and cooperation. Does not the horse have a soul? Your so-called horse whisperers can touch it. In nature, creatures understand cooperation. It is the human who fights the natural order, allowing ego to get in the way.

Do not fight the spirit within. Your body is along for the ride. It is Spirit which gives you freedom. You have the free will to decide if you will combat or cooperate. Will you dig in your spurs when Spirit nudges you or give it free rein?

## BEYOND THE SPOTLIGHT

Prominent names do make you sit up and pay attention. There are some who stand out as leaders and shine a special light. Others look upon these so-called stars with adulation. Why is this? For they see in that other a bit of what they feel they lack.

Why do you have your celebrities? For you humans do adulate those with many friends, much money, good looks, and popularity. Is it so enviable to be famous? You know this is not always so. Beyond the spotlight oft lies dysfunction and great unhappiness.

Shine the spotlight on your own life. All face dysfunction at times. All encounter unhappiness. Projecting your desires on another with supposed success takes you away from your own reality for a while, but you can only escape for so long.

The spotlight you need to shine is inside. Light up within by turning up the love. Respond to all with this most potent force and you will have no need to adulate others. There is no need to seek love and adulation when you know yourself as the source of love.

*November 16*

## YOUR MISSION

All of heaven rejoices when another spirit is welcomed back to the fold from their journey into human form.

It is always with uncertainty but the greatest joy that we send a spirit to experience life in physical form. The uncertainty comes from knowing that the truth of your identity will become clouded over by ego thoughts. Spirit will be hidden behind the veil of the body and its lower vibrations.

Will you fulfill your task of lifting the veil, or will you miss the signs along the way that say, "Awaken! Slumber no longer!" Remain not in the darkness, but remember why you have come. Turn up your light and love those around you. In this way, spark the memories of the place and state from which you come.

When you leave the body behind and return from this earthly mission, the intensity of your light will be the measure of how much you have gained. You add that gain—that increase—to the Whole, thus enriching all of Spirit. Quite a beautiful journey is this ongoing experience you call Life.

## CLEANSE

There are times in your life when you feel a need to escape. There is a nagging feeling that tells you that you need time on your own. Honor this.

You cannot help others all the time. You swim in a sea of vibration. The waves of those around you touch you and flow through you. This does affect your own vibration.

Get out on your own, if only to walk about for a short period of time. Sit in the silence on your own frequently. Take a bath. Yes, of course you do this regularly, but do this now with the intention of clearing your energy field. Envision the most pure, loving energy of Spirit washing through you, clearing away any vibrations which are not helpful to you. This "energy bath," taken on a regular basis, will regulate your emotional state and aid your physical health as well.

Do you see how you can minister to yourself when you treat each moment with awareness?

*November 18*


## THE GOLDEN EGG


The golden years. Why do you call them this? Gold is your most precious metal and holds much value. The golden years are a time to be treasured as well, for by this time you have unraveled many of the mysteries of this life you are living. The veil has lifted a bit.

For some, the later years are not so pleasant, filled with loss and the challenges of an aging body. Try, please, to tap into the sea of wisdom available to you once the veil lifts and see the body for what it is—a vehicle for the spirit. The spirit is far more precious than any golden trinket. You are that spirit, not the body.

Do not disparage the signs of aging, but welcome them as a sign that you have gained much wisdom and will go on to gain more still. Few lives are ever wasted. Some lift the veil higher than others, but in most cases there is soul growth.

This is the golden egg for which all search, the grand prize ... understanding finally who you are and that you never truly grow old.

## AT THE CENTER

There are times in your life when you struggle, and times when everything goes just right. At those latter times you wish that nothing would ever change, but in the back of your mind you wonder when the shoe will fall.

Life is like that, with its ups and downs. It is the Law of Life that all is like a pendulum swinging back and forth, back and forth, good to bad, happy and sad. Where is the line between two opposites? There is no clear delineation. It is all one experience arising from a state of pure "being."

Picture the arc of the pendulum as the path of your experience, then ride up the chain of the pendulum to the apex. Is this not the center of what would be a circle if the swing continued all the way around? There at the apex, in the center of the circle of experience, is stillness. And who holds the pendulum? The Great Observer.

You, too, can rise above the swaying, ever-moving arc of experience and rejoin the Observer at any time to experience peace. In this state of simply "being," duality disappears. You can rejoin your ups and downs at any time or simply choose to rise above them.

*November 20*

## WITHOUT ENVY

Jealousy is a human trait. There is no envy amongst those who know that all contribute to the whole. If another seems to have more happiness than you, or perhaps more toys, send them love. That which you send out comes back to you. Suddenly, you have happiness, and the desire for toys and self-importance goes away.

In sending love, you have activated the very Force which gives you life. Your spirit grows and expands, and you understand that all are here to learn to love. With such an understanding, there is no envy, only rejoicing that you are all in this together. Envy disappears as you understand that all of you need all the help you can get in helping others to see the Light.

## MORE THAN ENOUGH

There is more than enough love to go around. It is a fountain that flows from an endless Source. This fountain wells up within you and wants nothing more than to flow freely, to be expressed, and flow forth in every thought, word, and deed, for you are, *in deed*, the human source of love.

God is the Source of all love, and you are the physical manifestation of That. And so, we ask you: How could you be anything less than loving? It is only when your own thoughts stop the flow that you are less than your true self. You control the faucet. How to open it? Realize that Love is who you are in spite of what any other may have told you. You are Love at the core, here because you are loved.

You are, indeed, the chosen one—chosen to have this human experience and to express your true nature. Go forth today and in your deeds, in your words, and in your thoughts be naught but love. Oh, what a beautiful day awaits you now!

*November 22*

## LOOK UP

Lift your eyes to the sky. In so doing, you are activating the highest energy centers within the energy body. The physical act of looking upward is like a light switch. You need not open the physical eyes to do this. Merely shift your internal vision to the crown and the location of the third eye. There is an actual energetic shift that takes place.

After making this shift, say your prayers. Make your requests and give your thanks from this spot—the God Spot. Yes, God is in all places at all times, but with the consciousness deliberately shifted and focused in the location of the highest frequencies, it is far easier to attune to the higher energies which are always around you.

Yes, look up to connect with God, but not outside of yourself. Go within, where God resides—within all things ... within you ... for you are That.

## LIGHTENING THE BURDEN

Responsibility ... a feeling that you owe another something. At times it can feel like a burden, at others a blessing. Ego feels only responsibility to the self. Spirit knows that there is only one Self and that in serving others you are serving the greater Self.

From this vantage point, responsibility is seen as a blessing. The burden is lightened. Service to others. Can there ever be too much? In the human sense, yes, of course, for yours is a finite world with limits of time and physical abilities, so do not exhaust yourself.

As always, ask to be guided and simply serve from the heart in all that you do. Listen to the heart if the burden seems too heavy. The heart will always lead the way.

*November 24*

## BE THANKFUL

Holidays with missing friends. You are supposed to give thanks. You are surrounded by others who are celebrating, yet there feels as if there is a hole in your heart. You are so very used to the physical presence of loved ones who have passed that their absence leaves an ache.

Recognize this as a sign of how very connected you are at the heart and how very fortunate you are to have this connection ... this love. You will see them again, but it is not time. You still have living and learning and loving yet ahead. For now, fill that hole with loving, happy memories. It is you who chooses how you feel. Grief is part of the process of life, but you need not cling to it nor wallow in it.

If you could see your loved one over your shoulder, you would see them smiling and encouraging you to do the same. They are only a thought away. Be thankful for the family reunion you will enjoy again. For now, you are joined by love forever. May this thought bring a smile to your heart.

## SOURCE ENERGY

Love makes the world go 'round. Do you not have a song like that? And it is true. Naught happens in your world, including the rotation of your earth, without Love behind it.

Now, when you think of those things that are less than loving, look to the human mind and the choices ego makes. These are the result of free will--a gift from God. Are not at times gifts squandered? But if another can learn from the misuse of love, then all was not completely lost.

Look to the Cause of all you see and there you will find Love, for Love is the Source of all, and Source Energy is Love. You are That. You have Love, or Source Energy, as your cause, and that alone is cause for celebration.

*November 26*

## LOOK IN THE MIRROR

Worship. You know this word as one you save for your deities as well as for those you love dearly. You hold them higher than yourself in not only great esteem but a bit of awe.

Do you know that no one being is better than another, whether in human form or not, for all are of the same Source Energy? If you are to worship anyone or anything, then worship yourself. Ah, immediately ego puffs us and smiles, but it is not this aspect of the being to which we refer.

Worship the fact that you exist, that you live, that you are aware. This is the eternal self that exists in all of nature. You are Love, itself, walking about in a body for a while, but with or without the external covering you are worthy of worship. You need do nothing to earn this worship, but the more you can express and be the presence of Love, the more you will understand your true, innate value.

We love you so. Can you do the same for yourself?

*November 27*

## WAITING TO BE HEARD

Write down the words you hear when the Voice inside you whispers. What does it tell you to do? How does it advise you? What are its teachings? Do they make sense? Do they speak of love? How do they feel in your heart? Are you making them up? Is it your imagination? Can these words be trusted?

There is only one way to know. When the words feel right and when they will bring you no harm, act on them immediately and repeatedly. Soon you will learn discernment and trust. As your life takes a turn for the better and flows with a rhythm and smoothness never before experienced, you will ask yourself, "Why did I not listen sooner?"

Write down the words. It is not your imagination. How could Spirit speak to you, if not through the imagination? Trust us, your unseen helpers. We are here and we are waiting to be heard.

*November 28*

## WHERE WILL YOU FOCUS?

Distraction abounds in your world. You are contending with millions of egos, and all of them are clamoring for attention, most especially your own.

Where will you put your focus? You will place it on what you feel at the moment can best serve you, when you are coming from ego. What happens if you switch your allegiance to spirit? Your attention is drawn elsewhere.

Yes, colors do seem brighter when ego is put aside, but you also notice how many others could most certainly glow a bit brighter. Make it your intention to focus less on individuality, and more on the Whole. In so doing, you will see life in a (w)holy new light.

## SCHOOL OF MASTERY

The school of mastery--that is where you find yourself. Mastery of a job? Mastery of a task? Not at all. None of that matters at all in the end game.

Mastery of your emotions, my friends. That is the challenge you agreed to take on. How volatile are you? How reactive? Every response is a choice. You have been gifted with a brain in which the part that controls thinking is separate from the part that controls emotion. Did you know this? This is what we have been telling you now for quite a while.

You CHOOSE how you react and what you think. Therefore, how you FEEL from moment to moment is your choice as well. How can the soul grow in being more loving if you do not gain mastery over your thoughts? One step at a time is how. One thought at a time.

If you choose to.

# November 30

## WITHOUT THORNS

Every rose must have its thorns. They are protective devices, don't you see? The rose is so beautiful that the thorns keep away those who might grab them up by the bundles. But not all beautiful flowers have thorns.

What is it with the rose? It is there to teach you a lesson. Are you not attracted to roses? Are they not the symbols of love? Do you not give and receive them on occasions of sharing love? You are as beautiful as a rose inside and out, yet do you not project your own thorns at times, doing your best to keep others at bay? You have your protective measures, and you feel they are necessary.

Your florists cut off the thorns, and the roses are just as beautiful. Can you do the same? You are loved, thorns and all, but they are not truly necessary. In time, with evolution, roses will no longer have thorns, for they will no longer be necessary. May the same be true of you in this lifetime.

## COURAGE!

Courage comes in many forms. There is that which you know as bravery, when a human risks physical life to save the physical life of another. This is commendable. It shows selflessness.

But there is also the courage to be not like the majority of your humans in thought and deed. All of you are pure love and oneness on the inside, but few realize this and act from this place unconditionally. It takes courage to stand before a group who sees only separation and stand for love. Do you have what it takes? You all do.

Will you stand for love? There is no righteousness in doing so. There is nothing to prove, nothing to feel superior, angry or judgmental about in such an act of courage—merely the strong inner knowing of who you are and why you are here.

When others fail to see and exhibit love, may you have the courage to do so for them and for you.

*December 2*

Do not take your unseen guides for granted. Yes, they are there, but gratitude raises the vibration of all. Your gratitude is not necessary, but in expressing your thanks and acknowledging their presence, you strengthen the connection.

In asking for help you make the connection direct and instantaneous. We are here, always awaiting you, but is you who forges the link. Call on us at any time, but do call on us.

You are loved, you are guided, and you are never alone, but recognizing this consciously is always to your benefit.

## LAGGING BEHIND

All is intricately interconnected. The body is in rhythm with the rhythms of the earth and the other planets in your solar system. Even your moon affects your mood. How is this so? For all is energy.

When you are out of rhythm with the earth's energies, you experience a set of symptoms you label jet lag. There is dissonance and discord until you come back into resonance.

It is the same in your relationships. When you are out of sync with the vibrations of another, is there not discord? What about when you move into a new home or try to sleep in a strange place? Why are you uncomfortable? Your energy is not yet in resonance with the energies around you.

Be mindful of how the dissonance in your energetic field affects your human emotions. Be careful not to lash out at others or be hard on yourself while adjusting. Allow the confused waves to settle into a more peaceful rhythm and know that all will be well in time.

## December 4

### VIEWPOINTS

Is there not always an alternate way of looking at a situation? It is quite easy to bemoan your current circumstance. "Woe is me. Look how awful this is." And then, are your eyes not pointed toward one in a situation you would judge as far worse? And suddenly you are grateful for what you have.

At the same time, there may be another who looks upon you and is grateful they do not have to face your challenges. In experiencing what you are experiencing, you may be helping another. How you choose to see your situation is always up to you and is always relative.

Is there not always another way of looking at a situation? Infinite ways, my friend. We highly recommend choosing the one that brings the greatest peace.

## ASPECTS

"Defer" … "in deference to" … what does this mean? That you recognize something or someone other than yourself. You, on the spiritual path, are taught over and over that separation is illusion—that you are all connected—and this is true. But it is also true that the majority of your human life is spent focused on your individuality, for that is how you learn the hard way.

The so-called conscious mind appears separate. It is only when you rise to the sub-conscious and super-conscious that you are aware of your connectedness. This is where you access the guidance and insight you so often seek from others. We ask you to defer to that greater aspect of yourself (which, in truth, is not separate from yourself), and there you will find the answers you seek.

In deference to the ego, we daresay it does exist, but defer to the greater sight and insight of those aspects beyond the ego, and there, in this expanded state, will you truly awaken.

*December 6*

MAGIC

Magic ... it enthralls you as a child, for you have no explanation for the unexpected and inexplicable results. As an adult, you try your best to figure out the trick, sure that there is deception. Deception is a perception.

Magic is nothing more than the manipulation of thoughts and deeds for a specific outcome. And so, there can be black magic and white magic, dependent upon the desired outcome and the motive behind the so-called trick. Always we encourage you to use your thoughts for the greatest good, the highest outcome.

When you harness the magical powers of consciousness, you become a powerful magician. Use this power always to bring more love into your world.

## TRUE ALCHEMY

Alchemy … when you transmute a lesser metal into gold. How would you like to be an alchemist? We are about to gift to you the greatest tool of the alchemist: compassion. The lesser metals in this case are represented by such emotions as anger, judgment, and frustration. When you as the alchemist feel these emotions within yourself—for you see them in another—pull out the compassion. Spread it about liberally toward the other and toward yourself.

You would not be witness to anger, judgment, or frustration if love were fully present in your conscious awareness. It is always fully present, but must at times be transmuted from the lower vibrations. Love is the gold you seek, my friend.

When anger, judgment, frustration, and the like—the lesser metals— are present, transmute them into love—the gold—with the tool of compassion. Then, alchemy is possible. Now you hold the key. Go mine some gold.

*December 8*

## AMAZING YOU

You are amazing … just the way you are. Yes, these are lyrics to a song you know, but they bear repeating often. You sing your songs over and over, but do you tell yourself the words you most often need to hear over and over? Not enough, my friend.

You are amazing … an amazing child of God. Do not worry so much about self-improvement. Sit back, look in a mirror and see the amazing things we see in you. See through the eyes of God, not the ego who cringes at the mere thought of looking in a mirror.

Your every cell is amazing. Your body is amazing. Your mind is amazing. Your spirit is amazing. Why are you so critical? That is learned behavior. Do us a favor: Learn to see yourself the way we do. You are amazing … just the way you are.

## RELEVANCE

Salient …a word which means relevant. How is God relevant in your life? Is the Presence something you think about on a regular basis? How often do you focus on love and beauty? These are salient topics when referring to God. How often do you look upon a downtrodden one with compassion? … a salient emotion in the context of God.

God is ever-present in your life. You cannot escape the Source. You cannot deny the Force. Everything is salient when referring to the One True Power, for there is nothing that God is not. However, when your focus is on love, kindness, and compassion, you bring the greatest attributes of the self to Life, and then Love can dominate your thoughts and actions.

When Love is present in your consciousness, then everything else is irrelevant. Do not misunderstand us. It is not that nothing matters if love is not at the forefront, but everything else will simply fall into place. Why don't you try it and see? We are sure you will find our words have much salience.

# December 10

## GRATEFUL

All that is is energy. All expressions of life have their individual frequencies. Gratitude is one of the highest, with a match on each octave.

It matters not where you vibrate on a scale, when you express gratitude you rise to a higher vibration. Give thanks this day. Give thanks in every moment for Life. If you cannot find a reason to give thanks, give thanks for having the ability to reason. The act of being aware of your awareness and then giving thanks for it will raise your vibration. The higher the vibration, the more peace and happiness you will experience.

This is Truth. Find reasons to be thankful. They are everywhere. The more you recognize them, the more you are saved from ego's grasp.

## DOOR #3

When troubles get you down and you can see no way out, do not look out. Look within. "But that is the last place I want to go!" you cry. "I already spend too much time there, and it is a scary place."

This time, we advise you, do not choose Door #1 when you feel frightened and alone. Choose Door #3, where all comes together: body, mind, and Spirit – a holy trinity of sorts. There the All becomes the One, not in the solo mindset of the human, but in the infinite Mind of the Creator, of which you are a part.

Enter the peaceful stillness behind Door #3. You will find this doorway in the heart area, not in the brain behind Door #1. That one will oft lead you astray. Join us and all the help you will need at the heart center … deep, deep in the stillness of this safe and peaceful sanctuary.

*December 12*

## YOUR MOST IMPORTANT WORKOUT

The heart is a muscle you do not exercise enough. Allowed to lie dormant, it can atrophy. It is easy to forget what true spiritual love feels like if you allow your humanness to dominate. It is not that the human does not have the capacity to love; it is that so many have forgotten to live as a whole blended being of spirit and a free-willed human.

Exercise your heart with regularity. Focus on love no matter what is going on around you, and you will tone the most important muscle in your life.

## ETERNAL

All that exists is Consciousness expressed as waves of energy. You think you miss a person when they are gone, but what you are missing is their exact recipe of frequencies. Their body had a certain frequency that made it feel a certain way to you. Their eyes and nose and mouth vibrated in such a way that this made them appear a certain way to you. Their soul, especially, vibrated in a certain way that made them recognizable to you.

The body may be gone, but the soul lives on, vibrating, recognizable, eternal. You cannot destroy the soul, for consciousness continues. The body is recycled, as is soul energy, but the particular vibration that is your loved one will always exist in the ethers, as will you. It is all part of the greater Consciousness … all one sea of loving energy.

We return to this basic lesson over and over until it sinks in that you are all connected, all eternal, and All That Is at the core.

*December 14*

## LIMITLESS

Do you know the limit of your heart? Have you tried to find it? Try today. See if you can love too much.

When one is angry in your presence, open your heart more rather than closing it off for protection. When one is sad, open it even more and watch the healing take place. You are a healer. All of you are, yet so few realize this. Open your heart as wide as you can and stretch this muscle.

You have not even begun to realize the limits of love, for just when you think you have reached bliss, the heart expands again. Test the heart's limit today. Stretch it as far as you think it can go. We will meet you there.

## HANDS

You clap your hands to make a sound. This can be for various reasons: to call attention or to express appreciation or to keep a beat in time with music. Such versatility, and all this with two hands striking one another.

A hand strikes out and hits another being. Yet another use. These hands can be used for such a variety of means. They are instruments ... tools. They make noise, they perform work. They can strike a face or caress a face.

Who does the choosing of how these tools will be used? You do, of course. But do you not realize that you are an instrument of Consciousness? You can be used for harm, when will and ego get in the way, or good, when the greater Consciousness governs the instrument.

Be an instrument of peace and love today and every day, and that will be a reason for clapping.

*December 16*

## QUALITY NOT QUANTITY

You celebrate the years passed in physical form one after the other. You light candles and sing songs. 'Tis true, there is reason to celebrate life, but not merely life in physical form.

Celebrate existence. You consider the number of years in form important. You consider it a tragedy when one no longer has birthdays to celebrate. We see it differently. Celebrate the quality of the life. Celebrate the level of love and compassion-sharing achieved. This is something to sing about … another year wiser, another year more loving.

Quality, not quantity. This is what matters, for life goes on eternally. How long you spend in physical form matters not a whit. How you spend that time in physical form is what it's all about.

## BREATHE EASY

You, of yourself, can do nothing. You think you are autonomous, but you are not. You can try to hold your breath, and what happens? Aha! The body has a Mind of its own, does it not? Where do you think that Mind comes from?

You may want to continue breathing, but if the Mind that breathes you says, "Enough," then you will move on to another experience. So why do you struggle to have autonomy over your life? Relax. Surrender, even, and allow yourself to be breathed. The greater part of you has been doing a fairly good job of breathing you your whole life.

If your life is not going as you wish, perhaps there is a little struggle going on. Go into the silence and ask how you might have an easier go of it. There, when you are calm and the breaths come easily, you will find your answers. Once back out in what you perceive as reality, when the breaths are perhaps more constricted, you will have your indicators of how well you are listening.

## December 18

### REMINDERS

Yes, pain is a symptom that something is wrong. Likewise, emotional angst is a sign that you are out of alignment with your true nature. You can change both kinds of pain with your thoughts. The physical may take a while longer to catch up, but your emotional pain can go away instantly at the mere recognition that it is your thoughts which are the cause.

Immediately you will want to blame someone else. That is not the real you, but ego. The real you is hiding beneath the angst. Rise above the ego. Step into the role of the observer, the real you. See the transitory nature of the situation you are in. Now listen to what you are telling yourself that is causing your pain. How can you change the way you see this situation? Choose how you can best respond and find peace. It is always a choice.

We give you the same messages over and over, but do you not forget over and over to listen to your thoughts, your body, and your emotions? What is pain, but a reminder.

## YOUR MAJESTY

Nothing is insignificant. Everything you see exists for a purpose.

No one is insignificant. All are expressions of God. You are That. Do you feel insignificant? Look at a mountain. Feel its power. Sense its majesty. Now step into your new role, no longer a tiny, insignificant hill in your mind, but a tall, majestic mountain in the mind of the Creator, who creates nothing less than majestic expressions of Itself.

Express yourself today in all of your majesty and proudly claim your inheritance. Anything less is a disservice to the Whole of which you are a majestic part.

# December 20

## REACTIONS

"Did you meet the situation with love?"

This is the great test of your lifetime. It is a test you can apply after any event, any experience. And apply it you should, for it will be the question you are asked by your higher self and by those who gently guide you when you pass through heaven's gate.

Yes, your life is filled with challenges, and always you have a choice of how to respond. So many ways do you have from which to choose … with fear, anger, and defensiveness … by running away, by taking a stand, by doing nothing.

All is a spectrum from low vibration to high. Understanding this, you can see that the optimum choice is always love. We challenge you to find any circumstance when love is not the optimum choice. When faced with a choice, step into the future and look back upon the moment.

Did you meet the moment with love? Constant vigilance, my friend. Constant vigilance.

## UPS AND DOWNS

Every day presents new challenges with its ups and downs. Is this not just like your stock market? At times things are on an upswing, and at others there is a precipitous fall. We wish you to understand that all events are outside the True Self. You need not ride the ups and downs as if belted into the roller coaster. Instead, step back and watch the ride.

Yes, of course there will always be practical matters to attend to, for you are in this world. But never forget, you are not of it. You are a spirit-being having a human experience. Have your human experience, but do not become so consumed by it that you forget who you are.

When you find your emotions riding the same roller coaster as the events in your human life, then you have identified too closely with the human aspect. Take care of business, indeed, but let always a spirit of love and equanimity control the ride.

*December 22*

## CHOOSE PEACE

The universe does not conspire against you. It conspires <u>for</u> you. There are many who do not understand this. They have lived too long amongst those who use their free will as human beings for purposes less than loving. In those cases, they are going against the natural flow of the universe.

Were you to simply trust and relax, you would float instead of struggling upstream. When you surrender and trust, you flow directly into the main current of universal vibration and are swept up by it. Make this your intention—to flow with the universal current and be in harmony with it.

From this more peaceful state you will drift past those who are splashing and struggling. Extend a hand and invite them along, but be cautious of those who fail to surrender with you. Do not let them drag you down.

## EVER MORE BRIGHTLY

It is easy to become discouraged when you read your headlines. You work to bring more love into your world. You do your best to be the presence of love, to see only goodness, and in less than one minute a single focus of ignorance brings pain to many. One human being's use of free will brings down the vibration of others, drawing the world's attention to the fact that there is more work to be done.

Never forget that the power of Love will conquer evil. It is not a ratio of one to one, for every act of ignorance does not wipe out one loving act. The light of one self-realized soul is far more powerful than one who walks in ignorance. It is those very souls who realize that the self is spirit and not human who will shine ever brighter and hold the love and hope for others.

Why do you hold candles in your vigils? As a reminder that the light is still there. To light the way for those who cannot yet see through the darkness. Light a candle in memory of those who are now completely surrounded by love, relieved for a while of the burden of experiencing others' ignorance. As for you, shine ever more brightly now, candle or not, for you are the light, and shine you will eternally.

*December 24*

A LITTLE REMINDER

Glory on high from the highest … Do not forget God in all of this. Yes, focus on your friends and the joy they bring you. Focus on loved ones. Focus on your guides and angels and Jesus. But what of the highest Power? Where does God fit in? In the spaces in between; that is where.

God is in your friends and family and all of your helpers for sure, but also in every nook and cranny and space you can imagine, and even in those you can't. God is the all-pervading Force, the joy and the sorrow, the pleasure and the pain, the All That Is.

Give thanks to God. Give thanks <u>for</u> God, for without God, there is nothing. But even in the nothingness, there you will find God.

## A REASON TO CELEBRATE

"Happy birthday," we sing to you on this day in which millions celebrate the birth of one who brought a message of love, forgiveness, and hope. That hope still lives within you, that you will one day be saved. Saved from what? From mistakes you may have made? There is nothing to fear. You are already saved if you recognize that you are temporarily human and thus known to make mistakes.

Jesus brought a great message of salvation, that the Christ lives within. Not just one man had this power, but all creatures great and small. What is a Christ, but the being who awakens and realizes that he or she is eternally spirit, part of God, not separate at all. You are That! Yes, we repeat ourselves yet again, but is this not the perfect day to do so?

We wish <u>you</u> a happy birthday today as you awaken and realize your divinity. Now, how will you use this present?

*December 26*

## FLOW

Friends and enemies. Why do you categorize?

You do so because that is the human way. Unfortunate, is it not? But most instructive. Be aware that when you place others in a box you keep yourself in a box.

What if you saw others like water in a river, constantly changing as they flow through your life? Rather than resisting those you label as enemies, you let them flow by, realizing that all are part of the flow of life. There is great freedom in such a view, allowing greater peace to reside in your heart.

Be cautious of labels and allow all that is to simply flow.

## LIFTED

Surrender. It is not a throwing up of the arms and saying, "I quit." It is knowing that living in struggle is no longer your desire. It is knowing that you no longer wish to act alone and suffer.

Yes, raise your arms in surrender, but only like the little child who says to one who can help, "Please lift me up and hold me safely in your arms." As you are lifted, you rise above the drama. From this higher perspective, in the arms of Love, you can better choose how to react when you return to ground level. And as you return to walk around, you take a bit of that peace and Love with you.

Now, is surrender so bad?

*December 28*

## IN ABUNDANCE

Love one another. Take the attention off of the self and place it upon another. Now take what you would like to feel from that other and give that to them. Do you see? You did not really need love from them, for you already are that. You have it in abundance.

It is like your money. There is plenty of it to go around in your world, but some hoard it, some spend lavishly, while others experience lack.

If all realized that Love is your very essence and distributed it freely, it would flow equally. For now, simply practice allowing love to flow, with no expectation of return. You will be amazed at the result.

## PLAY ON!

Victory comes to those who stay in the game. It is always easier to step off the field and sit on the sidelines, but far more beneficial to participate. Yes, you would like to take a time-out from time to time, and that is quite understandable. It is also quite acceptable, unless you check out for so long that the body grows stiff.

Remain limber. Remain flexible. Stay in the game, but rely on your teammates for assistance. You are not a solo player, and you need not be the star. You are all equal players, all equally important. What is victory? It is the satisfaction that comes from having stayed in the game and having done your best. In that regard, all are winners.

Play on in this game of life. Give it your best, even when you get kicked around a bit. In reality, there is no score.

*December 30*

## A STATE OF MIND

Lonely is a state of mind. Why are some content to be found only with themselves, whilst others experience sadness and at times even panic when alone?

Go back, back, back in your personal history as a human, but only for your own enlightenment. We do not wish you to dwell in the past, but to visit it for understanding. What did you learn to tell yourself long ago that gave you the need for others' presence in order to feel safe? You are safe and loved now. This is one of your greatest tasks--to learn and know this.

Yes, it is delightful to be in the presence of those you care about, but you are deeply cared about at all times. Sit in the silence and ask to feel fully how very deeply you are cared for. These are not mere words. We pray that you will do so. Ask for this experience, and when your prayers are answered, you will begin to crave these sacred moments of silence when no other is around.

Seek balance between enjoying others and being alone, and never again fear loneliness.

## A FRESH START

A fresh start—that is what you are given today. "But our new year begins tomorrow," you claim, and do you see the artifice of time?

Why do you wait for a clock to tick or the page of a calendar to turn?

Make your new year, your new day, your new hour, your new moment this very moment. It is all you ever have, and it is right here, right now. What are you waiting for? If you are unhappy with any element of your life, happy new year! Begin to change it now in an instant with new thoughts.

The new year and the new you begin this very instant.

# Index

# ABOUT SUZANNE GIESEMANN

Author Suzanne Giesemann is a psychic-medium and metaphysical teacher whose messages of hope are presented with evidence and the highest credibility. She is retired from a distinguished career in the U.S. Navy which included duty as a Commanding Officer, Special Assistant to the Chief of Naval Operations, and Aide to the Chairman of the Joint Chiefs of Staff.

Suzanne has experienced one of the most unique career transitions ever – a career transition that spans dimensions. She captivates audiences world-wide as she brings hope, healing, and comfort through her work. Her gift of communication with those on the other side provides stunning evidence of life after death.

When Suzanne, her husband, Ty, and loveable long-haired dachshunds Rudy and Gretchen are not traveling and speaking across the United States and Canada in their motorhome, they reside in Central Florida.
*****
Suzanne shares the daily messages she receives from Sanaya on her blog at *www.SanayaSays.com*

Sign up to receive Sanaya's daily messages by email at: *www.SanayaSays.com*

"LIKE" Suzanne's Facebook page and receive Sanaya's daily messages directly to your newsfeed: *www.Facebook.com/SuzanneGiesemann*

Find more information about Suzanne and her work at: *www.LoveAtTheCenter.com*

Suzanne welcomes your comments and questions:
**info@SuzanneGiesemann.com**
888-692-0781 x1

CPSIA information can be obtained
at www.ICGtesting.com
Printed in the USA
BVHW040609241221
624768BV00003B/97